Who Owns *the* Learning?

Preparing Students for Success in the Digital Age

ALAN NOVEMBER

Solution Tree | Press

a division of
Solution Tree

555 North Morton Street
Bloomington, IN 47404
800.733.6786 (toll free) / 812.336.7700
FAX: 812.336.7790

email: info@solution-tree.com
solution-tree.com
Visit **go.solution-tree.com/instruction** for live links to the websites mentioned in this book.

Printed in the United States of America

16   16 17 18 19 20

Library of Congress Cataloging-in-Publication Data

November, Alan C.

  Who owns the learning? : preparing students for success in the digital age / Alan November.

     p. cm.

  Includes bibliographical references and index.

  ISBN 978-1-935542-57-5 (perfect bound) -- ISBN 978-1-935542-58-2 (library edition) 1. Student-centered learning. 2. Computer literacy. 3. Information literacy. I. Title.

  LB1027.23.N68 2012

  371.39--dc23

                         2012008985

Solution Tree
Jeffrey C. Jones, CEO
Edmund M. Ackerman, President

Solution Tree Press
President: Douglas M. Rife
Publisher: Robert D. Clouse
Vice President of Production: Gretchen Knapp
Managing Production Editor: Caroline Wise
Proofreader: Sarah Payne-Mills
Cover and Text Designer: Jenn Taylor

My two amazing children, Jess and Danny, have taught me to never underestimate the contribution that children can make to adding value to the knowledge of others.

Visit **go.solution-tree.com/instruction** for live links to
the websites mentioned in this book.

Throughout the book you will see this symbol:

These symbols are called QR (quick response) codes, and seem to be everywhere:
in advertisements, in magazines, on the back of T-shirts, on the windows of
businesses, and so on. They are powered by Tag Technology (to find out more
about this technology, see http://tag.microsoft.com/home.aspx). To access the
QR code, simply download the tag application on any smartphone or tablet.
Once you have downloaded the app, open the application and scan the code
using the camera on your tablet or smartphone. The app redirects the code to a
website using your web browser. The QR codes in this book will take you directly
to the websites being discussed for quick access to videos, blogs, interviews, and
additional support materials.

Table of Contents

About the Author

Alan November, MEd, is recognized internationally as a leader in education technology. He began his career as an oceanography teacher and dorm counselor at an island reform school for boys in Boston Harbor. He has been a director of an alternative high school, computer coordinator, technology consultant, and university lecturer. As a practitioner, a designer, and an author, Alan has guided schools, government organizations, and industry leaders as they plan to improve quality with technology. His writing includes dozens of articles and the best-selling books *Empowering Students With Technology* and *Web Literacy for Educators*. Alan was cofounder of the Stanford Institute for Educational Leadership Through Technology and is most proud of being selected as one of the original five national Christa McAuliffe Educators. He has worked with educators in all fifty states, Europe, Canada, Australia, Central America, and Africa. Every summer he hosts the Building Learning Communities conference (an event devoted to the concept of connecting and empowering children to lead more of their own learning and to contribute to the learning community).

Introduction

Have you ever stumbled across an idea or a seemingly random event that caused you to rethink the very essence of what you thought was true? I had just such an accidental insight, one that challenged my concept of the roles of learner and teacher and upended my understanding of the structure of schooling. It happened in 1981, when I was the director of an alternate school within Lexington High School, in Lexington, Massachusetts. It was the last Friday of the school year, and I had been summoned to discipline a student who was caught breaking into the school's computer lab. Nothing was stolen or broken, but the lab was part of my school and Gary was one of my students, so it was up to me to handle the incident.

Gary's crime mystified me. Yes, I understood his interest in computers, although I didn't share it—at that time, I thought computers were just dead machines filled with lines of code. But Lexington High School was a hotbed of computer science in the early 1980s. Many parents were in the computer industry along the Route 128 high-tech corridor, and Logo, the computer language developed for young children by the famous MIT computer scientist Seymour Papert, was piloted in Lexington. It was an amazing time and place, and educators from around the world came to watch our innovative classrooms. I wasn't surprised, therefore, by Gary's curiosity about computers. But why break in?

This student had never enrolled in a programming course (the only type of computer class offered at the time). He had shown no previous interest in technology and, in fact, had demonstrated little interest in school at all. He wasn't a troublemaker, but his performance was mediocre and his attendance record even worse. So why, after all of his friends had bolted from school for the freedom of summer vacation, had Gary broken back into a locked classroom, just to spend hours hunkered over a keyboard? That was just one of the questions I intended to ask Gary as I entered the computer lab to confront him about his break-in.

"What have you been doing in here?" I demanded as the first salvo in my riot act. Gary pointed at the computer screen before him, and then began scrolling through screens full of computer programming code. He said, "I've been writing a program." I had no idea what I was looking at, but I could tell Gary was proud of his work. I also could see that this student hadn't broken into the lab to vandalize it; he had snuck in to work on his self-taught programming skills. He broke into school to learn—not to earn credits, advance toward graduation, or gain teacher approval or praise. I had never seen a student so motivated, so self-directed, and so perfectly driven to learn (perfect except for the breaking and entering, of course). With that realization, I stopped thinking of ways to punish this student, and began thinking about how I could reward his drive. I was intently focused on helping all of my students to graduate, and I certainly didn't want to lose this one. I asked him, "What do you think about attending summer school and earning academic credit in a programming class?"

"I can't come to school this summer," he said. "I have a job as a mechanic at the Saab dealership." Then he added, "If you let me take a computer home for the weekend with all of the assignments for a programming class, I'll finish the work and bring it in on Monday."

Gary's suggestion seemed almost rude—an idea that defied the very structure of education as I knew it. He was going to complete an entire course in a weekend, with no teacher to direct him? I found the idea hard to swallow but decided to take a chance. I arranged for Gary to go home that day with a computer and a semester's worth of assignments from one of our programming courses. On Monday morning, Gary met me back at the school building to return the computer, along with all of the completed assignments. His perfect work earned him a C for the course—the highest grade he could earn without attending any classes. Clearly, the grade was not an accurate reflection of Gary's brilliance as a self-taught programmer. But Gary didn't care about the grade. He had taken incredible joy in setting his own goals and solving his own problems.

That experience completely changed my understanding of student motivation, the role of educators, and the potential for student-directed learning. It also made me realize for the first time that computer technology might have truly broad implications in the educational process. As Gary explained, the key to his success was that the computer provided him with immediate feedback about how his program worked (or did not work). Gary felt that he was fully responsible for the quality of his work (similar to the way students feel when they play video games). His observation of immediate feedback motivated me to try to understand how technology had the power to fundamentally empower students to own and lead their own learning. To launch that journey, I decided to design and teach my own computer course.

I began asking friends who were in the computer industry which programming language I should teach. One of my friends, a Harvard business professor named Roger Bohn, advised me to forget about programming. He told me patiently, "Software is coming. Very soon the whole concept of teaching programming will be outdated." If I wanted to understand the impact of computers in learning, then I should focus on using them to develop skills that remain useful no matter how dramatically technology evolves. He said, "My advice is to teach your students to learn basic problem solving."

And so, after a great deal of confusion, research, and revision, I developed a course called Community Problem Solving Through Technology. The course challenged students to identify a real problem in the community and find existing technologies that could help deal with it. I will never forget the meeting in which I presented the course outline to my department. My colleagues were as confused as I had been when I began my design journey, and the course focus on problem solving really threw them. They kept asking, "What kinds of problems will you give the students to solve?" and "What will your tests look like?" When I explained that my students would be responsible for finding the problems they would solve in the course, the response was universal: "It won't work." Eventually the department head came to the rescue and told my incredulous colleagues, "Let Alan develop his course. Let's see what he comes up with." If the students succeeded, so would I; if they failed, so much for my idea.

From the beginning, the course attracted a large student enrollment; students who wanted to use computers without having to learn programming signed up. The Apple II had just been released, and the first databases, word processors, graphic programs, and spreadsheets were hitting the market. At that time, there were no computer courses (other than programming) that I could take to prepare for my own teaching. Everyone I knew was self-taught. It turned out that as long as the motivation was there, learning about those tools was a straightforward process; you simply had to pick up the manual and go. To supplement my learning, I joined the Boston Computer Society and attended evening meetings where various folks would share their knowledge of computer applications. It was all very informal and very social. High school and college students were often teaching the adults.

It was just natural to extend my own learning from high school students in the evening at the Boston Computer Society to how I would organize elements of the high school course I was preparing to teach. I knew it would be important to empower my students to "learn how to learn." On the first day of teaching, I challenged my students to unwrap the cellophane on new boxes of software, pick up the manual, and go. I also encouraged them to learn from each other. Students were divided into teams to learn different applications. Students would then share their knowledge with each other. Looking back, this is really the only sane way I could have launched the first course so quickly. My students taught me a lot of the nitty-gritty details of how the software worked. It was a blast. My students enjoyed figuring out application tricks before I did. They loved teaching me, and I loved being taught by them.

The most difficult part of teaching was to guide the students as they identified a worthy community problem they could solve using the technology. While they immediately enjoyed learning how to use software out of a manual, they struggled with identifying their own problems in the community. I underestimated how unprepared they were for that task. One girl in first period summed it up: "Mr. November, *you* are the teacher. Giving us the problems is *your* job, not ours." Imagine one of the worst fears of teaching, giving students a challenge with absolutely no response. It was a Ferris Bueller moment: "Anyone? Anyone?" My colleagues' predictions of the impossibility of having students design their own problems were ringing in my ears.

To help break the paralysis, I invited various folks from the community into the classroom for student interviews. As these talks progressed, my class's excitement for the project grew. All of my students eventually identified community problems that could be solved with technology. In the process, they brought me some of the most rewarding experiences I have ever had as a teacher. Most astonishingly, for the first time in my career, some students wanted to continue to work on their projects into the summer vacation! I even had students who recruited friends who were not in class to help them complete their projects. I started to see that Gary wasn't alone; these kids loved working with technology. But I also saw that their drive was fueled by two important conditions: they wanted to have some ownership in the learning process, and they wanted their work to have purpose—they wanted to make a contribution even if they initially struggled with the challenge of identifying their own problems to solve.

Looking back, I can see that my friend Roger was right; programming is a very small part of what we teach in schools today. What none of us could have foreseen thirty years ago, however, is the way technology would permeate every aspect of our culture today. We didn't know then that many students would one day have access to computers, cell phones, and the Internet all the time (not just in school). We had no concept of social media, which has become a major tool for business, a driver of political and cultural change, and a critical communication tool for people of all ages. We couldn't have realized then the creative (and destructive) potential these technologies would offer all young people. From immersing themselves in Facebook and Twitter, to writing their own apps, to creating avatars and designing websites, today's students demonstrate a huge interest in creating and sharing content. Socrates was right: learning, for many of our students, is a social interactive enterprise. This book is based on the premise that given the right opportunity, tools, and teacher guidance, students want an equal voice in directing their own learning. It is possible that the structure of school as we know it has underestimated students' willingness to own more of their learning.

If Gary were in school today, he would not have to break into a computer lab to follow his passion for learning programming. He would just go home and log onto iTunes U, pick up an apps design course at Stanford (for free), and join a community of programmers from all over the world to share design ideas. His teachers would probably be completely unaware of how he is designing his own learning environment beyond the reach of school.

As Roger also rightly observed, however, if you don't know how to organize and solve complex problems, computer tools won't do you much good. In recognition of that important truth, I've spent the past thirty years building upon the experiences I learned in that first computer classroom to develop an educational model based on critical problem-solving skills, a model that leverages the powerful motivators of student ownership and purposeful contribution, a model that builds real and lasting learning even as it enables students to create a learning legacy for all students who follow.

I wrote *Who Owns the Learning?* to tell you about that model, and to tell the stories of teachers and students who have applied its techniques to solve real-life problems and make contributions to their community. While sometimes overcoming huge resistance from a staid traditional system, these teachers and students have joyfully expanded the traditional boundaries of learning to add value within their own classroom and the world. You will read stories of pioneering educators who have an absolute belief in their students' knowledge and imagination, teachers who accept their students' unlimited willingness to contribute to community as a basic truth. These stories cover a wide range of subject areas, come from around the world, and illustrate various tools that educators have used to make their vision (and those of their students) come to life. At the heart of all these stories is the key concept that students will work harder to achieve a purpose—designing a tutorial for their algebra class, for example, or a resource database for the handicapped—than they will for a grade. The people you will read about in this book are living examples of the educator John Dewey's (n.d.) belief that "education is not preparation for life; education is life itself."

Along with these stories, I've outlined a number of ideas for creating learning experiences that engage students by enabling them to contribute to the curriculum as well as to their community at large and, in the process, develop essential skills in problem solving, critical thinking, creative collaboration, and global communication. I call this approach the Digital Learning Farm.

Why the Digital Learning Farm?

In the past, when family farms were dominant, children were an essential part of the survival of the family. They performed jobs around those farms—caring for animals, repairing farm equipment, preparing goods to sell at markets, and so on—that were vital to the success of the farm and of the family. As machinery became more sophisticated, families began to use machines to perform those jobs instead, and children were required to attend school to prepare for the industrial economy. By necessity, teachers in rural one-room schoolhouses had to rely on older students to help the younger ones. As we moved to graded classrooms, this *teacher's helper* role was no longer needed once every student was on the same page in the same subject every day. We lost the value of children as contributors to the culture of school. Teachers became the central instructional figures.

The power of purpose and meaningful contribution has been missing from our classrooms and our youth culture for some time. While life outside our schools has changed dramatically over the past century, we cling to an early industrialized classroom model that often fails to encourage collaboration, innovation, a global work ethic, or critical problem-solving skills. Our students are caught in a process we call "cover the curriculum," regardless of their mastery of the material. We have inherited an organizational structure in which the teacher owns and manages the learning. This industrial model underestimates the natural curiosity of students to direct their own learning; they have little opportunity to contribute to the design of the learning process or find a sense of greater purpose in their work. One high school student I interviewed summed up the traditional model this way: "The most important skill to have to succeed in school is a willingness to learn how to be taught." Contrast this observation with the highly valued skill in the global economy of "learning to learn." As Harvard researcher Tony Wagner shared with me, "The essential skill of the 21st century is knowing how to ask the most interesting questions" (personal communication, November 2011).

Today, very little of the work we give students in school provides them with a sense that they are making a contribution to anything other than their own educational progress toward graduation. Indeed, once the grade is recorded, a huge amount of student work is thrown away. It has no more value. Now that we have powerful, easy-to-use design tools and a capacity for worldwide publishing, we have an opportunity to restore the dignity and integrity of a work ethic with redefining the role of the learner as a contributor to the learning culture.

Unfortunately, the opportunity that technology can bring to our students to help them lead their learning has not been leveraged. In too many cases, we bolt new technologies on top of current learning tools in the standard learning environment, which effectively means that we give our kids a thousand-dollar pencil. In other words, we teach students to use computers to create papers or do other work that could have been done without a computer. I have watched students in laptop schools simply use their devices to take notes while a teacher lectures. Too many of our elementary students are still memorizing the fifty state capitals when they could be building interactive digital maps of the history of state capitals.

The tools we have today can help us craft a new vision that empowers our students to own and lead more of their own learning. The goal of the Digital Learning Farm model is to redefine the role of the learner as a contributor, collaborator, and leader in the learning culture. In many of the examples in this book, you will see that teachers have given students one of the most powerful motivators of high-quality work: purpose. Imagine a school where every learner is valued for making a contribution to benefit the whole class. The questions (1) Who owns the learning? and (2) Who works harder in the classroom, the teacher or the student? drive the thinking behind the solutions described in this book.

The jobs we can create for our students can encompass everything from researching curriculum content to creating and publishing learning tools to collaborating with students and other content providers around the globe. As more powerful digital tools become available for free or little cost, the opportunities for our students to apply these skills will only continue to multiply.

In the Digital Learning Farm model, students supply much more of the creative design, preparation, delivery, and revision of the educational process, enabling teachers to spend more time in the roles of mentor, advisor, and facilitator. As a result, responsibility for the quality of the work shifts to the learners. Students can become more engaged in the learning process; they do more, they think more, and they learn more. They also have an opportunity to build their own educational legacy by creating content that will spur ideas for new learning experiences long after the original creators have moved on. Perhaps the most amazing transformation takes place in the classroom. Students work harder than their teachers. Teachers learn more about the learning styles of their students and have more time to individualize instruction. Many teachers report that the Digital Learning Farm model leads to a savings of the most precious commodity for teachers: time.

While traditional education doesn't emphasize the goals of contribution, purpose, and problem solving that lie at the heart of this model, these goals are in exact alignment with the skills our students need to thrive in today's global workplace and economy. Here are just some of the ways everyone wins with the Digital Learning Farm model:

- Students develop essential 21st century skills in empathy, self-direction, innovation, communication, and collaboration.

- Teachers gain more control over their time and can devote more attention to personalizing instruction.

- Student thinking becomes more visible to themselves and to the teacher.

- Parents gain better and more immediate insight into their students' educational progress and projects, and have more opportunities to view and experience student work.

- School systems gain access to proven technology educational programs without having to make major investments in new technologies. As you will see, most of the student work described in this book involves very little in the way of equipment and software, and even students without at-home computers and online access can participate.

- Society gains a new generation of lifelong learners with a strong work ethic, a critical understanding of how to use technology to solve problems, and a well-developed sense of global empathy that enables them to communicate and collaborate with people from any geographic area or culture in the accomplishment of tasks and goals.

The Digital Learning Farm model represents a shift of control. Much of what used to be teacher directed in the traditional model is powered by students in the Digital Learning Farm model. Adjusting to this kind of shift can be difficult. I met a teacher who told me he had adopted the model and his students were working harder than he was. Then he said something that stunned me: "I have to wonder if I'm earning my salary." I told him that if anything, he should be paid *more*. He had created a culture of learning that empowered his students to dramatically improve their work ethic and encouraged them to develop the habits of curiosity and exploration that mark lifelong learners. In the Digital Learning Farm model, the role of the teacher is more important than ever.

The revolution has begun. All over North America, pioneering teachers have led the way in implementing ideas that leverage the capabilities of their students to take a more active role in the learning process. In this book, you'll read about a number of these bold educators, including:

- **Eric Marcos**—His middle school students in Santa Monica, California, have energized their school through the use of podcast tutorials. These students record themselves solving problems based on material and methods they've discussed in their classrooms, and they then upload the videos to the web. Under Eric's leadership, these students have created an online library of video tutorials that can be accessed and used by anyone around the world.

- **Darren Kuropatwa**—He is a high school calculus teacher whose daily scribe program is just one way in which he has transformed his classroom into a collaborative learning community. In that program, one student is assigned on a rotating basis to take notes for everyone in the class. The student scribe receives immediate feedback on the notes from Darren, and then posts the approved notes on the class blog for everyone to use. Struggling note takers improve with immediate feedback and practice, and students who never took notes in the past are now doing so, knowing that peers are depending on them.

- **Garth Holman and Michael Pennington**—They are middle school teachers from two schools in Ohio whose students collaborated to create an online world history textbook written *by* students, *for* students. The wiki is still collecting visitors and updated content from students around the globe.

As you read the stories of these and other educators, you will see that the processes and ideas of the Digital Learning Farm model revolutionize the role of every player in the educational system. Students take on the role of contributor and content provider, teachers become mentors who help guide the process and drive home the lessons it teaches, school librarians help students learn to navigate vast collections of information and even publish their own resources, and superintendents and principals support educational innovation and help lead the transition to new models of learning. My hope is that the ideas and techniques outlined in this book will help educators everywhere find their own opportunities for creating new examples of the Digital Learning Farm model in action.

Getting the Most From This Book

Who Owns the Learning? is a guide as well as a collection of student and educator profiles. It's about ideas (some of which are already being put to use in classrooms) and the concrete methods and techniques any educator in any school system can use for implementing them. In the first chapter, I'll talk more about the Digital Learning Farm and the role of students, teachers, principals, and even school librarians in maximizing its success. Chapters 2 through 5 each focus on a specific type of work for students on the Digital Learning Farm—tutorial designer, student scribe, student researcher, and global communicator and collaborator—and look at examples of that work in progress. Each of those chapters will include these core elements:

1. **The Story**—These real-world examples illustrate how students are tackling and defining this type of work in classrooms across the United States and around the world.

2. **Tools and Techniques**—You can use these technologies to leverage this type of work in the classroom. I'll also include information about which packages are free, what commercial software is available, and how to set up and organize these tools. You'll also find essential information about classroom management, the pedagogy to accompany the software, and next steps for teachers and principals.

3. **Questions for Discussion**—I'll end each chapter with questions that can help educators and study groups explore the chapter topic and its role in implementing the Digital Learning Farm model, including questions

about maintaining balance and control between teachers and students, determining who introduces new concepts, and managing the transition to this new model.

In chapter 6, I will share with you a real-world example of the power of student contribution. There we take a close look at the work of two teachers who have employed the full range of student jobs described in this book in their middle school world history classrooms. These students have built a life-changing educational experience and created a legacy that will long outlast their student years.

Throughout the book, I'll share with you the stories gathered in more than thirty years of classroom work and educational consulting, in conversations with experts I have interviewed in my online learning series, and in my seminars and workshops with educators from around the world. I encourage you to remember that these examples are illustrations, not rigid instructions, and that you can find ways to use the information you'll gain in this book in any setting. You can look at work being done in a sixth-grade class and find specific and direct ways to incorporate it into strategies for your first-grade or eleventh-grade students. Just as I'm encouraging you to let students stand on your shoulders to find new challenges and create new ways to meet them, I urge you to use the information in this book as a foundation on which you can stand to find your own answers and opportunities. After all, the most successful way to teach students innovation and creativity is to embrace those elements in our own methods.

Welcome to the Digital Learning Farm

1

My own experience with students making a contribution to community began in the winter of 1976 when I was a high school science teacher in the Boston Public School system. I leased an abandoned barbershop for a dollar; the shop was on Dudley Street, in a row of storefronts tucked below an overhead subway station. The city was going to relocate the station, and all of the buildings below it were scheduled for eventual demolition. In the meantime, the city of Boston auctioned them off for temporary use. My one-dollar bid for the barbershop was a winner!

I had been inspired to bid on the barbershop by an odd twist of fate, a medical emergency that brought together my roommate (a medical student) and one of my own students, a sixteen-year-old boy. My student had been taken by ambulance to the hospital where my roommate was a resident. The boy had no medical records and had not seen a doctor in years. My roommate was frustrated that the boy's family had failed to take advantage of the free medical care available in clinics across the city. He urged me, "Please teach your students how to access Boston's free clinics. This kid could have avoided his crisis completely if he had walked into a clinic weeks earlier and been treated before his ailment became serious."

When I read about the Dudley Street subway auction in the paper, I imagined the barbershop as the perfect headquarters for a community health information center. Location, location, location! Along with thousands of other Boston commuters, I passed that space every day as I got off the Orange Line subway and walked the few blocks to Roxbury High School. It was where many of my students hung out in the morning and after school. I knew the intimate scale of the barbershop with the original leather chairs and marble sinks would make a wonderful space for a health information center. But would my students get as excited as I was about converting it to a community resource? Excited enough to volunteer their work? I soon found out.

Immediately, students signed up to paint the outside of the barbershop. We chose a hideous lime green so it would stand out. The students scoured the local neighborhoods, gathering brochures about medical services. They cleaned the place up and organized brochures along the counter next to the barber chairs. Students who never did their homework and often skipped school showed up for their volunteer work. Unlike my classroom experiences, many of my students worked harder than I did in our health information center. The time they spent there was fun and productive. No grades, no assessment; just honest work to make a difference in the community.

The barbershop was a magical place where I learned as much as my students. Perhaps my most valuable lesson came from seeing the transforming power of authentic work for students who were traditionally unsuccessful in school. I realized that many students work harder to achieve a meaningful purpose than to earn a grade. I also realized that by giving students an opportunity to make a contribution, you can see them in wonderful new ways—how helpful they are, and how kind, considerate, and attentive they can be.

Not too many generations ago, young people were expected to engage in work with purpose—caring for farm animals, repairing equipment, selling food at local markets, and helping to care for younger children in the family. These responsibilities taught children the value of hard work and a strong sense of accomplishment.

Over time, mechanization eliminated much of the need for child labor. Gaining an education became the primary responsibility of most young people; they were not expected to be productive members of society until they entered the workforce as educated adults. Today, we rarely expect young people to be contributors. Few young people have opportunities to pursue work that has a purpose. I think that is a terrible loss for our society as a whole, but I also think it doesn't have to be that way.

Just as mechanization reduced our dependence on child labor, advancing technologies have brought us full circle in the potential for purposeful work among school-age children. Social media, mobile devices, and other information and communication tools enable students to make contributions to their classrooms and their communities and to extend the benefits of those contributions across the globe. As educators, parents, and leaders, it is our responsibility to give students the opportunities to put these capabilities to work.

The Digital Learning Farm model does just that. It leverages inexpensive and easy-to-use technologies to challenge and support more active participation of students and to give them more ownership in the educational process as tutorial designers, scribes, researchers, global communicators and collaborators, and more. This approach restores the dignity and integrity of the child as a contributor, even as it teaches students skills that will help them compete with peers from around the world. Pioneering teachers across the United States are adopting the Digital Learning Farm model by taking technologies out of the project mold and making them a fundamental part of the learning experience, and by giving students rigorous and more motivating assignments that prepare them to become more productive in our new global economy. These educators are helping their students leave a lasting legacy within their learning communities. It's an exciting time!

In this chapter, we'll take a closer look at the Digital Learning Farm model and some of the educators and students who are pioneering its methods. We begin, however, with a brief overview of the big-picture issues driving the need for this model, including the shifts in the culture of work that are triggering the need for changes in our culture of learning. We'll walk through some positive steps we can take to reframe our educational structure to support the type of self-directed, collaborative educational model represented by the Digital Learning Farm. Finally, we take a look at the roles of everyone involved in this model, from superintendents and principals to teachers, librarians, and students. I will describe four student jobs within the Digital Learning Farm and some of the creative ways students who do this work are making valuable contributions to their learning communities. While educators can implement any of these jobs individually, the stories offered in this chapter will illustrate that these jobs help create a balanced approach to teaching and learning and enable teachers *and* students to work smarter.

Drive and Purpose

In his best-selling book *Drive*, author Daniel Pink (2009) points out that the most important predictors of high-quality work are autonomy, mastery, and purpose. How well does our traditional educational model promote these three elements in our students' lives? We typically blame students for being unmotivated and for underperforming, but many of our students have very little autonomy and are rarely allowed to direct their own learning. As for mastery, many students have little opportunity to master subjects; the curriculum is covered, and the class moves on.

Purpose may be the most important of Pink's three predictors of quality when it comes to daily school work. Beyond earning a grade, many of our students see no higher purpose in their work efforts. Yet nearly every educator you will read about in *Who Owns the Learning?* says that their students often ask for—or willingly produce on their own—extra work, *when they believe that work has purpose*.

What if we could apply autonomy, mastery, and purpose to the learning culture for every student? That is the goal that drives the Digital Learning Farm model; to create a culture of learning in which students feel autonomous, masterful, and purposeful.

A New Culture of Learning for a New Culture of Work

We hear a lot about the technology revolution, but sometimes much of what we hear misses the point. While we often focus on the growth of social media and Internet access, technology's most profound impact has been on the very concept of work. Information communications technology is completely reorganizing how, where, when, with whom, and even why people work. This global cultural evolution is redefining our notion of jobs; as a result, we see an emerging enterprise-centered workforce in which workers manage their own businesses and sell their services to many different customers across a globally connected market. In his book *Strategic Planning in America's Schools*, William Cook (1995) observes: "Truly educated people of the next century will not apply for a job. They will create their own" (p. 32).

The transformation of the workplace that Cook describes is well underway. As best-selling author Thomas Friedman (2005) notes in *The World Is Flat*, we live in a world where work can move overnight to anyone who is connected to the Internet and can provide the work cheaper, better, faster, or all three. The move to in-home offices has boomed. High-performance workers need to be self-directed and interdependent. Learning how to learn is an essential lifelong skill. Global empathy is a critical skill for anyone hoping to identify global opportunities and secure foreign markets and customers.

This new work culture isn't limited to white-collar workers. At John Deere, welders have moved from a traditional workplace format in which they were told what to do and when to do it, into a format in which they strategically direct their own work. Using information and communication technologies, a John Deere welder in Moline, Illinois, can connect in real time with another welder in Germany, and together they can collaborate to solve problems and become more proficient at their work. In the words of one welder, "I no longer park my brain at the gate before I come into the plant" (personal communication, October 1993).

If technology is turning the industrial concept of the highly managed worker into a social artifact, how should educators prepare students for this new economic and cultural reality? Simply adding technology—the thousand-dollar pencil—to the current highly prescribed school culture won't help very much. Ironically, that common educational approach has served to freeze the industrial model of work in place. I have visited contemporary laptop schools that, for the most part, look and function exactly as they did in 1981 when I began teaching with computers. Successful implementation of technology into K–12 education is much more complex than providing students with access to computers and moving content to online courses. Instead, we have to teach students to use information and communication technologies to innovate, solve problems, create, and be globally connected. By enabling students to drive aspects of their educational experience, shape their involvement within it, and seek higher purpose by making educational contributions that benefit others, we can bring our educational approach in alignment with the changes in the global workplace.

The Digital Learning Farm model offers just such an approach. It rebalances the control of learning, giving more of the control to learners. The technology infrastructure, while essential, isn't the central issue in the educational process. Instead, technology is simply the means that makes the process possible, by giving educators, students, and parents opportunities to adopt new roles and relationships.

The Digital Learning Farm model changes the culture of learning, giving students much more responsibility by encouraging them to be collaborators, contributors, and researchers. At the heart of the model are ideas that address essential questions for educators: Who owns the learning? How much autonomy can we afford to give our students? How much purpose can we design into school work? And how can we design learning environments that lead to mastery? See table 1.1 to see how the Digital Learning Farm model compares to education's traditional model.

Table 1.1: How the Digital Learning Farm Compares to the Traditional Educational Model

Traditional Educational Model	Digital Learning Farm Model
It features the same prescribed assignments and rubrics for all students.	Students design more of their own assignments and rubrics.
There is an audience of one (the teacher).	It has the capacity for a worldwide, authentic audience.
Reward and punishment are external (in the form of a grade).	There is opportunity for more intrinsic rewards.
Student work is not leveraged to help all students learn.	All students contribute to the learning processes of the entire class and to learners around the world.
The critical skill is to know how to be taught.	The critical skill is to learn how to learn.
The limit of learning is what the teacher already knows.	Students research content beyond the teacher's knowledge.
The curriculum is covered regardless of students' mastery.	There are more opportunities for mastery.
Students rely on their teacher for help.	Students rely on their teacher and the whole class for help.
Parents have limited access to day-to-day student creativity.	There is an increased opportunity for parents to see creative student work.
Technology reinforces the current industrial culture.	Technology is used as a transformational tool to change the culture of teaching and learning.

Unlearning is more difficult than learning something new, and one of our most important challenges is to let go of existing structures in order to build more effective ones. We still have too many schools that focus their planning efforts on technology instead of on information and global communications. That technocentric focus does not create new models of learning; it merely bolts new tools on top of the current learning environment. By focusing on information systems and the flow of communication, we can define and develop a new educational framework. Then we will be better able to look beyond technology in our search for ways of collaborating for and with our children as we help them become independent, critical leaders of their own work.

Reframing the Educational Structure

The Digital Learning Farm model represents an educational environment that can foster the skills and qualities that embody the autonomy, purpose, and mastery students need in order to succeed

continued →

in a global economy and thrive as lifelong learners. Adopting it will require some remodeling of our current educational structure, though. Here are some important steps for building a framework to support the Digital Learning Farm model:

- **Increase the autonomy for students**—By giving students more responsibility for designing their own homework, in-class projects, tutorials, curriculum content, and even the methods by which they're assessed, we can engage the students' attention and energize their participation in the educational process. As a result, we can achieve better learning, create a more pleasant educational environment, and get more benefit from the time educators spend in preparation and presentation.

- **Publish student work to a global audience**—We should expect all students to create knowledge products and publish them for authentic feedback. For examples of this process in action, look at Kathy Cassidy's first-grade blog from Moose Jaw, Saskatchewan and Eric Marcos's sixth-grade math tutorials at Mathtrain.TV from Santa Monica, California. Visit http://classblogmeister.com/blog. php?blogger_id=1337 to read Ms. Cassidy's blog.

- **Create a community of contribution within the classroom**—We have amazing new tools for linking student projects so that every student's work has the potential to benefit all learners. Check out the notes from Darren Kuropatwa's calculus students from Winnipeg, Manitoba, which we talk about in detail in chapter 3 (page 39).

Starting at the Top: Redefining the Role of Superintendents and Principals

Any successful organizational evolution relies on strong leadership. In adopting a new educational model, superintendents and principals must lead the way. I can't overstate the importance of the role of a leader in setting policy, modeling the learning process, and encouraging expanded learning opportunities for students, teachers and school administrators—all critical elements in building a solid foundation for learning in a 21st century school environment.

Eric Williams, superintendent of the Yorktown School Division in Yorktown, Virginia, is convinced that principals who use digital resources in their own work make better role models for teachers and students in the Digital Learning Farm model. One way that he helps introduce educational leaders to these resources is through what he calls the *Digital Playground*. Unlike a traditional technology workshop, the Digital Playground is a monthly gathering that gives principals a chance to play around with the kinds of tools and technologies being used by students in the classroom. There are no formal presentations, but principals from throughout the school district get together and learn how to play with emerging information and communication tools that their students are using. They might learn, for example, how to post news on a school website rather than writing and distributing a weekly newsletter. By opening up to the innovative and creative possibilities of digital tools, these leaders can find better, more enjoyable ways to do their own jobs, while at the same time, serving as a role model for everyone engaged in the educational process. Conversations also include opportunities for transforming learning. Eric has made a commitment that all principals should foster a professional culture that encourages teachers to support student contribution.

Superintendents and principals must lead the cultural evolution of education by establishing an expectation that supports self-directed professional growth and more collaboration among teachers, not just within their school community, but globally as well. By doing so, they set the tone for teachers to create learning environments that bring these same qualities to the classroom.

James Tracy, headmaster of the Cushing Academy in Ashburton, Massachusetts, along with his educational team, breathed new life into their school library by rehabilitating the space into a vibrant microclimate for individual study and the collaborative exchange of ideas.

To reposition Cushing as a K–12 incubator school, James and his team began treating the academy as an entrepreneurial school. In that context, they had a series of meetings about what to do with the library. The large space was grossly underutilized; in fact, surveys found that students weren't using the library for research purposes at all. Instead, they drew information from online sources—often unreliable ones. James and his team decided that rather than continue to maintain the book vault library, they would put their money into a database that would provide access to peer review journals and other reliable sources, and then teach students the value of utilizing these sources (rather than citing information that came from a blog someone was running out of his or her mother's basement).

James's next challenge was to find a better way to use the library space. Surprisingly, he found a model that made sense for the school's new library in an open, collaborative space at the Google offices in Mountain View, California. Following that model, Cushing took out bookshelves and turned the library into a common study and interactivity space. In addition to quiet cubicles for individual study, the library had spaces set up for students to work in groups of two or more—what James calls "microclimates of interactivity." The spaces offered multimedia interactive displays, monitors, and so on, so students could access and shape information in ways that furthered their discussion. Next, the school moved the faculty mailroom into the library so every teacher would have to go in there every day. As a result, there was more use of the library, more collaboration between students, and more interaction between students and faculty. "It's a huge success!" says James. "There are more students in the library than any other room on this forty-three-building campus at any given time" (personal communication, January 2012).

With so many more students using the library and with so much more information available from it, Cushing had to add another full-time librarian to its staff. The students recognize the need for librarians now more than ever, because they're faced with an information overload that they haven't had to grapple with before. They're also learning advanced techniques for digital research using legitimate, verifiable sources. Librarians now work flextime, so one of them is always available for student questions via texting and email. Today, the library at Cushing Academy is accessible anywhere, anytime—and so are its librarians.

Transforming the School Library

The school librarian plays a critical role in helping the faculty and students transition to the Digital Learning Farm model. Every library can become a global communications center where students connect with partners around the world to collaborate and create work, and to present that work to authentic global audiences. Librarians can also be critical resources for their colleagues by helping other educators learn how to connect with classrooms around the world, and learn how to guide their students in these collaborative processes. In chapter 4 (page 49), you will learn more about the innovative ways librarians are helping to reshape the educational culture and student work on the Digital Learning Farm.

Standing on Our Shoulders: The Role of Teachers in the Digital Learning Farm Model

As stated previously, the Digital Learning Farm model represents a shift of control in the educational process as students take more responsibility for designing and implementing educational experiences. Rather than diminishing the importance of teachers, this shift makes their role even more critical to the educational process. Rather than simply focusing on the transfer of knowledge process, teachers in the Digital Learning Farm model guide students in the complex tasks of innovation and problem solving, and in doing work that makes a contribution to the learning processes of others. While teachers remain responsible for ensuring that the curriculum is covered, student contributions to the learning experiences deepen their understanding of curriculum content.

Teaching in the Digital Learning Farm model doesn't require a strong command of specific technical tools and skills; instead, it leverages educators' ability to tap the underestimated value of student contribution. Teachers continue to ensure that student work is meeting expectations and that there is clear evidence of student learning, but they also empower students to be more autonomous and more collaborative. For example, teachers may create assignments and in-class activities, while student-generated content helps the class master material. As Eric Marcos's library of student-generated math tutorials exemplifies, not only do students in this model help others in their class, but their work can help students from around the world and in years to come. As you are reading this book, there may be dozens of students from around the world learning math processes by watching tutorials on Mathtrain. TV (you will learn more about Eric's class and its work in the next chapter).

One of the most important tasks for educators adopting the Digital Learning Farm model is finding the right beginning. Often that means identifying a single project that the teacher can work through with the class, one that spawns new ideas for new learning experiences. The stories you will read about in this book provide plenty of fuel to begin the journey; the energy of discovery will drive educators and students to continue creating new goals and finding new directions. Leading the transition to this model can be fun—but it's still a transition. That transition involves changing our understanding of student motivation *and* our expectations for student contribution and collaboration.

Consider this: when my son Dan was in high school, he used five basic tools for managing his self-created content (music and writing), communicating with the world, and accessing entertainment: Facebook, his iPod, Instant Messenger, YouTube, and video games. Of course he also had a cell phone, which he would often sneak into school. (I knew this because every once in a while I would receive a text message from Dan about his day.) Otherwise, in school, he had no access to the tools he loved to use. In fact, he was taught that they have nothing to do with learning.

At home, he chose his applications and easily moved from one to another. He was self-taught, self-directed, and highly motivated. He was locally and globally connected. But it is safe to say that Dan was not as engaged at school. He was not valued for being self-directed or globally connected. For instance, he wasn't allowed to download any of the amazing academic podcasts available, from "Grammar Girl" to "Berkeley Physics," to help him learn. When he was studying the American Revolution, he was not connected via Skype to students in England, which might have created an authentic debate about the American Revolution's origins that could have been turned into a podcast for the world to hear. His assignments did not automatically turn into communities of discussion in which students helped each other at any time of the day. His school successfully blocked these tools from campus. In fact, in many schools, educators label these effective learning tools as hindrances to teaching.

What do schools accomplish by blocking students from learning how to use social media as tools for learning and educational contribution? Yes, these tools can be disruptive to the highly structured learning environment of the traditional school. But what if we could have the best of both worlds? What if we could use the allure of Facebook, Twitter, YouTube, and other similar tools to empower students to be autonomous, masterful, and purposeful in their academic work? Clearly, when students leave the filtered environment of school and make their own decisions about using social media, they are choosing to create content, to collaborate with friends, and to be globally connected.

If we could embrace the tools many school districts are blocking (which are also essential tools for participating in the global economy and culture), we could build much more motivating and rigorous learning environments. The Digital Learning Farm model gives us an opportunity to co-opt the tools our young people want to use, and reframe them as potent engines for driving a more meaningful educational experience. With that shift, we would have an opportunity to teach the ethics and the social responsibility that accompany the use of such powerful tools. These tools can be a major distraction from learning or they can be a major catalyst to it. Our students will benefit from the pioneering educators who work with students to explore the power of these tools and, in turn, empower students to be lifelong learners and active shapers of a world we cannot yet imagine.

Owning Their Learning: Student Jobs on the Digital Learning Farm

Perhaps the greatest role shift in the Digital Learning Farm model is that of the student. As we help to transform students from passive receptors of information into active drivers of their educational experiences and designers of their educational goals, we need to provide them with the incentives of meaningful work and authentic audiences. Here are the four types of jobs for students that we will discuss in this book:

1. Tutorial designers

2. Student scribes

3. Student researchers

4. Global communicators and collaborators

Tutorial Designers

Students often learn better from other students; they listen more intently, understand more completely, and participate more readily. Using webcams, video software, and other freely available recording and broadcasting tools, students can create tutorials that other students, parents, and viewers can access and use from any location. As you will learn in chapter 2 (page 25), teacher Eric Marcos and his students from Lincoln Middle School in Santa Monica, California, have energized their school through the use of screencasted tutorials they produce. Creating tutorials increases student engagement and provides struggling students with more opportunities for reviewing troubling concepts. As one of Eric's students reminds us, "In order to teach it you really have to learn it" (personal communication, December 2011).

Student Scribes

Not all students take excellent notes every day, but free online collaboration tools can give any class the opportunity to collaboratively build one set of perfect notes. Using a shared blog, wiki, Google Docs (http://docs.google.com), or another collaborative writing tool, students work together to create a detailed set of notes that can be used by the entire class. (Visit **go.solution-tree.com/instruction** for live links to the websites mentioned in this book.) Darren Kuropatwa, a high school calculus teacher, uses this student scribe technique to transform his classroom into a collaborative learning community. In chapter 3 (page 39), you will learn more about Darren's student scribe program (http://tinyurl.com/68djoz) in which each day a new student is responsible for taking notes and collecting diagrams that become part of his class's online calculus textbook. Using a student scribe program encourages students who don't take notes to do so, and it helps students who struggle to take good notes improve their technique through positive feedback and advice from their teachers and peers.

Student Researchers

Many classrooms have one computer sitting in the back of the room or on the teacher's desk that gets very little use while instruction is taking place. What if that computer became the official research station where one student each day was responsible for finding answers to all the questions in class—including the teacher's questions? Assigning students the research job can be a very effective learning tool, and it's an incredibly simple process: each day, assign a different student to sit by that computer. When questions come up during class, it is that student's responsibility to search out the correct answer. In chapter 4 (page 49), you will learn details about using this student job to build a class search engine that meets course standards for curriculum content and reliability of resources. Training students in the role of researcher offers guided opportunities and teachable moments that allow them to hone their research skills.

Global Communicators and Collaborators

It wasn't that long ago when it was cost prohibitive to have your class connect with other classes and subject experts around the world. That time is gone! In an ever-shrinking world, we now have free access to make these very connections. In chapter 5 (page 65), you learn how educators are using Skype (www.skype.com) and other online tools to establish and maintain working relationships via the Internet with classrooms and topic experts from around the world. (Visit **go.solution-tree .com/instruction** for live links to the websites mentioned in this book.) Students can develop questions, conduct interviews, and build their skills in online learning and collaboration with people from different countries and cultures. This Digital Learning Farm job offers hundreds of opportunities for any adventurous group of students to bring the world into its classroom.

These jobs offer just four examples of work that gives students valuable opportunities to make real contributions to their learning community. While educators can implement these and other student jobs individually, we can create a more balanced approach to teaching and learning by bringing multiple jobs together to work in harmony. I have talked with educators who assign different jobs to their students. If the work results in meaningful activities that advance student contributions and ownership in the learning process, it probably deserves a place in the classroom.

Taking It Home: The Role of Parent Support

We should also acknowledge the role of parents in making this educational model work. We have seen that under the Digital Learning Farm model, students take on a number of new jobs—taking notes for an entire classroom, documenting research, interviewing outside resources, recording and posting those interviews on class blogs, and more. Students working in this environment often do a number of jobs that in the past their teachers would have done. All of this means that parents may very well see their children spending less time on traditional homework and more time on creating content that benefits other students.

As I mentioned earlier, the Internet is one of the most powerful tools for involving parents in the education process. By enabling parents to visit the classroom and view student work through communication technologies, teachers provide parents with a means of participating directly in their children's education, no matter how busy their schedule or how long their commute might be. Because much of the work students do as scribes, reporters, and content providers is posted online, parents also will be able to see and use the work their children are producing. And as the Digital Learning Farm model builds skills in teamwork, students will be better able—and more willing—to partner with their parents and teachers in completing projects and accomplishing their educational goals. This educational transparency also enables parents and teachers to collaborate more fully in tracking and discussing student progress, attacking problems as they develop, and helping students remain engaged in learning. Indeed, there are wonderful stories from Digital Learning Farm classrooms where parents are as active in watching online tutorials as their children. Think about all the parents who don't know math well enough to help their children with it; in the Digital Learning Farm model, parents would be able to sit with their children and review tutorials produced by other children.

Of course, the digital divide remains a serious problem, as many students still do not have access to computers and other technology tools in their homes. This is a problem that we must address as a society if we want our students to thrive and remain competitive in a global economy that demands technical savvy. However, many educators are finding ways to make these learning opportunities available to everyone in their class, whether or not they have a home computer and online access. In some schools, librarians are given flextime, and the libraries are open before and after school.

Strengthening the Bridge Between School and Home

Building stronger collaborative ties between educators, students, and their families requires a communications infrastructure that links every teacher and every family to the Internet. But the paybacks of that infrastructure more than outweigh its costs. In addition to giving educators, students, and families a more accessible means of communication, this kind of network can also serve as a vital source of information. I recommend that schools set guidelines for teacher contributions to the school home page that include:

- Frequently asked questions from parents

- Goals for every course

- Examples of past students' work

- Recommended homework assignments for the entire year

- Hot-button connections to other sites on the web that support learning

- Action research projects

Balancing Responsibility, Shifting Control

While the majority of educators whom I have met support the concept of children owning or leading more of their own learning, the move to the Digital Learning Farm model can be a very difficult transition. As I learned in my own teaching, students initially can be very uncomfortable when asked to accept more responsibility for their educational materials and processes after years of having their learning managed for them. Some teachers report, for example, that their students have to adjust to the idea of taking notes that will be used (and reviewed) by their peers. Educators may need to adjust to this model too, as some of the responsibility for introducing ideas and techniques shifts to students (rather than remaining solely with the teacher). Parents may also question why their children are spending hours designing a math tutorial for one problem, rather than using that time to do ten problems at the end of the book. After all, they may wonder, isn't building instructional material the job of the teacher? Even when faced with this initial resistance, however, every teacher I have spoken to who has made the transition says it was well worth the effort.

With all of those shifts in control come some amazing changes in outcomes as students and educators benefit from the motivating drives of autonomy, mastery, and purpose. Once students realize that they are valued for their contributions to the learning community, it is not unusual for them to add examples to class notes, or to add a link to a tutorial, or to have extended conversations outside of class about subject content.

Today, I could do the community resource center project I told you about earlier in this chapter, without the one-dollar barbershop. I'd teach the kids to organize a website containing a Google map tagged with all of the city's medical services. Students could capture digital images and videos and geotag locations with their cell phones. They could add a list of services and interviews with personnel with links to the site listings—all in multiple languages—which could bring critical health-care information to tens of thousands of city residents. Each year, a team of students could update and maintain the website. If I had to, I bet I could link the site content to core curriculum in biology. And I doubt that my students' test scores would suffer from the depth and detail of this purposeful work. The project would be different than it was thirty years ago, but it would be right for the 21st century classroom, with more relevant activities for our students and better outcomes for them and the community at large. It would be a project that the student authors could show off to their friends and family wherever there was Internet access. Their grandmother might make good use of the website to locate important medical services. It may even motivate other students around the world to want to build a similar interactive health resource map for their region.

Our approach to education must evolve along with its tools, processes, and outcomes. We are already experiencing a cultural shift toward collaboration and learning empowerment in U.S. schools, as we realize that we must go beyond testing to have students demonstrate that they own their learning experiences and can apply the knowledge they have learned.

Questions for Discussion

1. As an educator, do you anticipate resistance from students as you ask them to make more of a contribution to the benefit of the class? How might parents react to this shift?

2. What first steps might you take in building a learning community where your students take on more responsibility for contributing to the learning of the class?

3. What evidence have you seen that corroborates Daniel Pink's assertion that autonomy, mastery, and purpose are the elements of true motivation and, therefore, indicators of high-quality work?

4. Do you agree that we need to fundamentally change the culture of teaching and learning to make better use of the powerful tools of information and communication technology? How could you begin that process?

The Student as Tutorial Designer

2

If you question whether students are truly willing to do the work necessary to make real and substantial contributions to the learning experience, consider the story of Jasmine, a student in Eric Marcos's sixth-grade class in Santa Monica, California.

One afternoon, Jasmine's mother was surprised that her daughter was not waiting in front of the school for her usual ride home. When twenty-five minutes had passed, Jasmine's mother went into the school to look for her. She stopped one of her daughter's friends who was on her way out the door and asked if she knew where Jasmine was. "Yeah," the girl said, "she's in the math room working on a tutorial for the class." Jasmine's mother headed right to the math room, where she found her daughter totally focused on adding music to the intro of what looked like a movie about solving some kind of math problem.

Jasmine's mother said, "What are you doing? I've been waiting in the car for thirty minutes." The girl briefly glanced up before looking back at her work. She said, "Sorry, Mom, I have to get this right. Everyone in class will be able to use this video to learn how to factor with prime numbers. I need another hour. Can you come back then?"

Jasmine's mom was confused; since when had her daughter become so diligent about math homework?

I understand this mother's confusion. If you had asked Jasmine how long her math homework usually took, she might have said, "Oh, about seven minutes." Yet she spent just under three hours working on the tutorial. What is the difference? As Jasmine later told me, her tutorial *really* mattered—not just to her or her teacher, but to her classmates who could use it to help understand the math problem it illustrated. Jasmine also was quick to say that she benefitted more than anyone else from her tutorial work because "in order to design a good tutorial you really have to learn the math."

Not only does Jasmine's work contribute to the knowledge of other classes in her school, but it also contributes to the learning of students around the world. As I wrote the draft of this chapter, I sat in my home in a little town called Marblehead, just north of Boston. It was early Sunday afternoon. I had just visited the Mathtrain. TV website that publishes Eric's student tutorials, where I captured the visitor list you see in figure 2.1. As the figure indicates, during an hour-long time frame, the site was visited by learners from Vermont, North Carolina, Georgia, California, Liverpool, and Switzerland. The math tutorials on this website are popular around the world and viewed by visitors at any time of the day or night, throughout the year. All of this content was produced by eleven- and twelve-year-olds under the guidance of their sixth-grade teacher.

Recent

11/13 @ 12:23: Marblehead, Massachusetts, US
11/13 @ 12:23: Sanford, North Carolina, US
11/13 @ 12:11: Switzerland, CH
11/13 @ 12:11: Chicago, Illinois, US
11/13 @ 12:20: Liverpool, GB
11/13 @ 12:06: Fremont, California, US
11/13 @ 12:04: Huntersville, North Carolina, US
11/13 @ 12:01: Raeford, North Carolina, US
11/13 @ 12:00: Statesboro, Georgia, US
11/13 @ 11:45: South Burlington, Vermont, US
11/13 @ 11:36: Maple, CA

Figure 2.1: This list details visitor activity on the Mathtrain.TV website.
Source: Copyright © ClustrMaps Ltd., 2012, www.clustrmaps.com. Used with permission.

Students teaching students is a powerful method for building learning and driving creativity and innovation. With easy-to-use tools for screencasting and publishing to the web, students have a 24/7 opportunity to engage in peer tutoring with children from other classrooms, schools, nations, and cultural backgrounds. Of course, Eric Marcos (like other teachers whose students take on the role of tutorial designer) provides guidance to ensure that tutorial content is accurate, and he offers feedback to help students design, organize, and edit their work. But Eric doesn't grade them on their tutorials, which may be another strong motivator for his students. As author Daniel Pink (2009) explains in *Drive* (2009), the more we grade creative work, the less of it students will do.

If you ever have a chance to log onto Mathtrain.TV and watch some of the tutorials to the end (they average about three minutes in length), you will hear many of the young authors say something like, "Thanks for listening." These kids are grateful for the viewers who use their work. And for many of these tutorial designers, their global platform and worldwide audience provide an even greater motivator to do good work than would any grade they might have received.

Later, we'll take a close look at the value of students teaching students, as demonstrated by the work of Eric Marcos's class and other student tutorial designers. In the process, we will talk about the technology these students and educators use, and the ways they incorporate it into the overall learning experience in the classroom. We also will explore some basic techniques for guiding students as they create and publish learning tutorials.

What if we have underestimated both the students' need for help in learning and students' willingness to provide that help to others? Do you believe that students who need help with learning material will ask the teacher for assistance? If they do ask, consider the enormous drain on the teacher's time all of that individual instruction would entail. Students who are lucky enough to have the right friends can ask them for help. In fact, students have told me that the help of their friends can play a big role in determining their own academic success. What if we did not leave the social peer support to chance but made it fair and accessible for all students? As many teachers and researchers know, peer tutoring (when managed well) can be one of the most powerful methods for improving learning. The emergence of easy-to-use creative tools can empower every student to become a contributor to the ecology of the classroom.

One of the emerging roles of teachers is the role of global publisher of student work. Eric Marcos has accomplished just that by publishing his own students' tutorials and thereby making them available to everyone in class for the current year and every year to come. As new students experience the tutorials published on the website, they in turn are inspired to design their own.

Designing and publishing their own tutorials gives students a sense of ownership, autonomy, mastery, and purpose. At the same time, placing students in the role of tutorial designer improves their learning outcomes and enables their teachers to spend more quality time personalizing instruction during class. Using student tutorial designers also gives teachers an opportunity to gain a better understanding of the learning styles of their students. If you peruse Mathtrain.TV, you will see many different styles of tutorial designers. Some students team together in a two-person radio show format. Others use music or colorful graphics. These various creative approaches give teachers invaluable insight into how students are thinking about content and how they develop mental models of processes.

Eric Williams, superintendent of the Yorktown School Division in Yorktown, Virginia, has seen the benefits of students teaching students, firsthand. One middle school math class within his division, for example, has created Animoto videos to teach math skills to other students. Go to www.animoto.com/education to learn more about making videos with this site. (Visit **go.solution-tree.com/instruction** for live links to the websites mentioned in this book.) One student designer put together a tutorial on two-step equations, and another focused on lessons in converting fractions. These tutorial designers referenced textbooks and online resources, then used their notes to create the tutorial content. They were determined to get it right because they knew their video tutorials would be viewed by peers, both in their school and outside it.

That class wasn't alone in its use of student tutorial designers; Eric told me that another teacher in his division was preparing to help her students create poetry podcasts for sharing with others via smartphones and MP3 players. In another school division, an autistic high school student designed a tutorial in algebra, too. While he may have a lot of difficulty working in a one-to-one peer tutoring experience, this student can produce tutorials on a Promethean board with a professional approach. Imagine how his world has opened up through his ability to make a contribution to the learning experiences of others!

Brad Ovenell-Carter, head of the THINK Global School (which you will learn more about in chapter 5) also witnesses the educational power of student tutorial designers. Brad explains how incredibly effective student tutorials can be for teaching concepts that can trip up students, especially those that include a detailed review or represent a new idea the class hasn't encountered before. "I'll kind of run through it once," Brad says, "and then nominate a couple of kids to put something together that explains the idea, or the method, or the skill that the other kids can use." That explanation goes on the school's wiki as part of a tutorial data bank that the students can access.

Teachers at the THINK Global School have found that this growing data bank has helped improve the quality of their teaching time. "If you have a student who needs just a little reminder," Brad says, "instead of having to stop and explain it, you can say, 'Go have a look at this; if you're still stuck, come and see me.' That frees up a huge amount of time for the teachers to do the more interesting stuff and keep the conversation going."

Those are just a few examples of the growing recognition of the educational benefits of giving students ownership and purpose in the learning process. These examples also illustrate the incredible motivating force of preparing work for an audience that extends beyond a single teacher, a single class, and a single school. To put it plainly: give students a real audience, and they will do real work. Now let's take a close look at one of the best examples of this student job in action.

The Story: Student Tutorial Designers Power the Mathtrain

As you have seen, Eric Marcos and his class at Lincoln Middle School in Santa Monica, California, are pioneers in creating and publishing student-designed tutorials. Today, universities are using his class's website, Mathtrain.TV, to help train teachers to take advantage of student-created learning tools. And it all began with one video, produced to help one student, a girl who calls herself Paul (all students were asked to choose an alias for their online presence for privacy reasons), who was struggling with her homework.

Here is how Eric explained it: "I was at my house, and I got a message from Paul saying, 'Mr. Marcos, I don't understand problem 37 on the homework tonight. Can you help me?' At that time, I used email to help students outside of class. It can be really difficult sometimes to explain a math problem through email, with all of the little symbols and power signs and whatnot. But I had just gotten a tablet PC, and I had run across this Camtasia Studio software for producing videos. So I made a quick little diagram on my tablet PC, and I explained the problem and recorded the whole thing with Camtasia Studio. It took me a couple of minutes, and then I made it into a video file and emailed it back to my student. Within less than an hour, she had an explanation for her question. She watched it and wrote back to me something like, 'Thank you for the video. Now I understand it. Could I have another one?'"

That was how Eric began laying the tracks for the tutorial website that his class created and named Mathtrain.TV. Eric's student watched the video, understood the problem, and became very excited about the whole process. That stoked Eric's excitement, too, so he began posting the tutorial videos online, where the entire class could access them.

At that point, another student—a girl who calls herself Bob in her tutorials—approached the teacher after class one day and said, "Mr. Marcos, can I make one of those videos?" Eric was surprised but thrilled to give her the go-ahead. Bob created one of the class's first student mathcast videos, in which she talked about proportions. According to Eric, Bob "really, really set the precedent for all the other videos that would ever follow."

Bob quickly learned how to use Eric's tablet PC and the Camtasia Studio software. In her video, she introduced herself and the topic she was going to explain, and then began sketching out the problem of proportions on the tablet as she walked through the solution. She signed off by saying, "Thanks a lot for listening, and goodbye!" Her presentation was well-organized and easy to follow, with a clear beginning, middle, and end—just as she had learned to compose information in her English class. As Eric says, "From that point on, we've been pretty much copying her style."

From the very beginning, it was obvious to Eric that the student tutorials had great teaching power: "When I showed those first student videos, the kids responded in an amazing way. I guess I should have known that they would love to watch their peers explaining how to do proportions or how to do cross-multiplication." The students not only loved watching the videos, but they wanted to make them—lots of them.

After collecting a library of student tutorials, Eric launched Mathtrain.TV, a YouTube clone website where his students share all of their student videos. The class also has created and released iTunes podcasts, which are another way to organize and publish tutorials in a searchable format. Today, Mathtrain.TV has attracted a global audience. Although Eric hadn't envisioned the site's success, he hasn't been surprised by the tutorials' broad popularity. See figure 2.2 (page 30) to see a visual representation of online visitors to the Mathtrain.TV website.

Eric sees that students really respond to hearing their peers deliver information in an authoritative manner, but using *their* vocabulary and language style. As he describes it, "Maybe some students just like that it's a kid who's explaining it, and it makes them think, 'Oh, I should be able to handle this and understand it, too; it's no big deal.'" The ability to pause and replay the explanation at any time also helps students learn deeply from the tutorials. The tutorials are helpful for parents, as

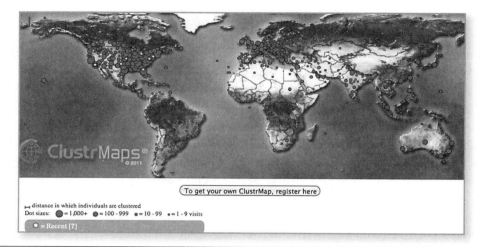

Figure 2.2: This is a screenshot of a cluster map showing online visitors to Mathtrain.TV from around the world.

Source: Copyright © ClustrMaps Ltd., 2012, www.clustrmaps.com. Used with permission.

well, who can use them as aids when they're helping their kids with math homework or as tools for brushing up on their own math skills.

Eric Marcos has had a number of new sixth-grade classes enter his classroom since he first began the student tutorial project. So how does he—or any other educator leading a class that includes student tutorial designers—manage and contribute to the growing library of video tutorials produced over the years? What happens when the students have done it all? Does Eric toss out all of the preceding year's entries in order to allow his new students the opportunity to create a tutorial on a subject that's already been covered by a previous student's video work on Mathtrain.TV?

"No way," says Eric. All student videos remain on the site, where they can be viewed again and again over the years. He goes on to say, "We have no problem making more than one video on the same theme." In fact, having multiple perspectives on a single subject can be a powerful learning aid, and every kid may have his or her own take on the best way to tackle a problem. Eric, however, gently suggests alternative topics when a student asks to do a tutorial on a subject that's been covered multiple times: "I might try to say, 'That's cool, but you know, no one has made one yet on factorization or distributive properties.'"

It's important for educators to remember that tutorial designers are engaged in a creative process. That means that most of them won't want to repeat someone else's idea, and they prefer to be the first to take on a given topic. As Eric says, "Unless they really feel like they can do something different and innovative, they usually like to try to find that niche or that topic that nobody has done yet." See figure 2.3 for a screenshot of the Mathtrain.TV website.

How does this type of student work impact the learning and teaching process? As Eric and other pioneering educators have discovered, student-created tutorials carry enormous educational power for everyone involved in the process. Teachers watch how their students explain ideas and gain insights into the way young minds

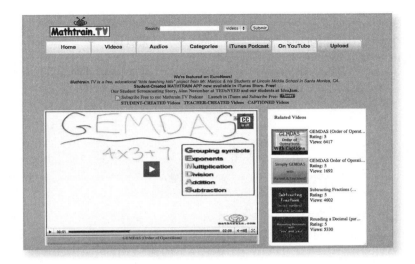

Figure 2.3: This is a screenshot of students teaching students through Mathtrain .TV tutorials.

Source: Copyright © ClustrMaps Ltd., 2012, www.clustrmaps.com. Used with permission.

perceive those problems. Eric's experience, for example, gave him a new understanding of the elements of mathematics with which his students struggle, the work-arounds they might use, and even the gaps in understanding that can go undetected in class or on tests. Most importantly, in guiding them through the production process and watching the results, Eric gets to know his students in a deeper way than might otherwise be possible. "I love telling people that we've got kids that come after school and hang out for hours in a math classroom," he says. "People usually roll their eyes and go, 'You're kidding me.' Middle school math, and these kids hang out for hour. For me, personally, that's been great."

Because student tutorial designers generate so much excitement around their class topics, they create a better atmosphere for learning and teaching. The process breeds creativity and innovation, even as it encourages students to become more invested in a successful learning experience. That means that they do their homework more carefully (and regularly) and participate in classroom discussions. The tutorial design process also helps students build important skills they will use for the rest of their lives, including planning, communicating, and collaborating, as well as mastering important information and communication technologies.

How the Students of Room 208 Conquered the World

When Bob Sprankle began teaching at Wells Elementary School in Wells, Maine, he inherited the school's only non-computer-lab Internet connection. Using freely available blogging software, Bob's combined third- and fourth-grade class launched its own educational

continued →

blog and began posting student-produced podcasts of interviews, discussions, tutorials, and other learning events. Soon comments began
coming in from students and educators around the world. The international conversations that resulted became a motivating force within his
classroom and a trailblazing example for educators everywhere. The
series, which ran from 1999 to 2006, was cited by technology and educational leaders for its groundbreaking achievements in 21st
century skills education. Although the Room 208 blog is no
longer active, you can visit www.bobsprankle.com/blog
/index.html to view it (and the student podcasts).

The Room 208 students became pros at fielding questions from
teachers and classes in Japan, Switzerland, and other places in the
world. "At first it was like wow, wow!" Bob says of his students' reac-
tion to this experience. "Then they just saw it as a norm, that this is
the 21st century, we communicate globally, and we're not alone here,
learning alone. It's a real community out there."

The podcasting project quickly proved to be an incredibly powerful teaching tool. Bob says, "When I did my direct teaching for a
five-minute lesson about a grammar rule, 80 percent of the students
were not listening. Who wants to hear that? But when we worked
on our podcast, they were very invested in grammar because they
knew they had to get it right. They saw themselves as professional
writers." Bob's role developed into that of guide and mentor as the
students took more responsibility and control over their learning process: "Most of the stuff they had to edit or fix, they would identify
themselves. Maybe I had to name it, like, 'Yes, that's the subject-verb
agreement we were talking about,' and then they would go off and
fix it. I really saw my role change drastically."

Bob sees individual students gain confidence and the whole class
grow stronger as a result of students' work as producers of teaching
content. The students easily entered into online conversations with
educational blogger David Warlick and other professionals
who contacted them in response to the podcasts (see
http://davidwarlick.com/2cents/). "What a confidence
builder!" Bob remembers. "They just saw themselves as
co-teachers and right in there with the global work that was being
done." The Room 208 students produced and presented a film about
the creative process to the Maine Technical Learning
Institute (see www.bobsprankle.com/blog/C1697218367
/E630200618/index.html), were featured in an article on
Apple Computer's website, and became accustomed to
newspaper interviews. Bob says his students took their fame in stride:

"They just saw that this was part of their work. They had already found purpose to everything they were doing. They had listeners and this was part of learning—people engage with you and carry on the conversation."

According to Bob, other teachers who are interested in podcasting should begin with a class blog to introduce students to the idea of interacting with a bigger world. The blog also provides the essential platform for posting content. "From there," Bob notes, "it really comes down to the question of what do we want to share; what is meaningful to us?" Answering that question is a good exercise for students, and it can be an intense experience for teachers. Quickly, however, everyone involved will discover that creating teachable content can occur anytime, anywhere. "It could be a field trip." Bob remembers. "It could be a book discussion. It could be turning on the recorder for five minutes a day and sharing that. It doesn't have to be a heavy production, just something that you want to start a conversation about with other people." (Since leaving Room 208, Bob has been active in helping other educators develop programs aimed at preparing students with 21st century technology skills. He still maintains his own blog, called Bit by Bit, where he offers a forum for teachers who want to learn about podcasting. You can visit http://bobsprankle.com/bitbybit_wordpress/to read the blog.)

Tools and Techniques: Working With Student Tutorial Designers

Fortunately, teachers don't need to have a broad command of technical information or a large bank of equipment in order to introduce this student job into their classroom. You can create student tutorials like those on Mathtrain.TV with these three simple tools:

1. A tablet PC or iPad with ScreenChomp installed, a Wacom interactive tablet, or an interactive whiteboard with its built-in screencasting software

2. An inexpensive microphone (you can use the mic that came with your computer, but even a relatively inexpensive external mic gives better sound)

3. A copy of Camtasia Studio or Jing video recording software (both are available online at www.techsmith.com)

Using Basic Screencasting Equipment

If you have an interactive whiteboard in the classroom, you're all set up to record presentations. Whether you work with one of these devices or a tablet PC, the act of recording your written and verbal information in a screencast presentation is quite fluid and seamless. You can just have the students sit at a desk, start the screencasting software's record feature, and draw their prepared presentation illustrations on the tablet PC or interactive whiteboard as they speak their prepared text.

Really, Really Basic Tools for Creating Student Screencast Tutorials

What if you don't have the money for a tablet PC or interactive whiteboard? If you have a single computer in your classroom, you can produce some very basic student video tutorials. Simply open up a copy of Paint, Tux Paint, or MacPaint—any kind of drawing program that you already have or can download free online. The results may not be as polished as those you can get with an interactive writing tool, but they'll work.

Next, download a free copy of the Jing screencasting software, and prepare to record the verbal instructions that go with your written work. Again, you can use the microphone that came with your computer. Follow the instructions for starting your recording, and as you record your explanation, use the mouse to write or point to onscreen objects such as numbers, charts, and so on. When you finish the explanation, hit the Stop button on Jing and the program automatically converts your recording into a movie file. You can then email the file, show it in class, or post it on a website. (Please note that the maximum length for Jing videos is five minutes.) I suggest that you ask a student to learn how to use the software. Within a day or two, he or she can help teach the software to the teacher and classmates alike.

Wacom tablets, which look like blank slates with an interactive drawing pen, are a less-expensive option than a tablet PC for creating the screencast tutorials. Plug the electronic slate into your computer, and then draw on it with the pen. Your drawing is displayed directly on your computer screen, which enables you to use your computer like a tablet PC. Many designers use these tools, and when combined with Jing software, they make a great screencasting setup for a very modest investment. The professional versions of the screencasting software cost more, but they give you more editing options and enable you to save files in better file formats. Visit http://bobsprankle.com/podcasts/0506/rm208vodcast.mov for a wonderful guide to the podcast process, and a great example of a student-created tutorial. (Visit **go.solution-tree.com/instruction** for live links to the websites mentioned in this book.)

When I talk about this type of project with educators, they often ask me about the equity issue, or how it works for those children who don't have Internet access, an iPhone, or other device for viewing video tutorials outside of school. In those cases, educators and their student tutorial designers can simply burn the screencasts onto a DVD for viewing on a home or library computer. In fact, Eric Marcos told me of a group from North Carolina, the Free Linux PC Program (also called FLPC), who have downloaded Mathtrain.TV videos onto DVDs, loaded the tutorials onto refurbished computers, and then have given the computers to needy families in their community. The costs of technology are continually decreasing, and free wireless Internet access is becoming more widely available, so we can anticipate that the costs involved in creating, publishing, and viewing student-designed tutorials will shrink over time.

As the community of viewers for student tutorials grows, educators might find that the exposure helps bring in new resources for funding ongoing projects. Even though many of Eric's fellow teachers at Lincoln Middle School had no idea for some time that he and his class were publishing video tutorials for a worldwide audience, others in the community were paying attention. When the chairperson for the math committee at the school learned about the project, he began watching the student videos and fell in love with the project. He persuaded the PTA to donate money for buying PCs and Camtasia Studio software for every math teacher in the school. That gift has given a boost not just to student tutorial designers, but to all students who now can use and interact with the new technologies. Now more teachers at Lincoln Middle School are using their new equipment and software to launch student tutorial projects just like Eric's in their own class.

Taking Cues From the Students

I had an amazing opportunity to interview some of the tutorial designers from Eric Marcos's math class. Some are current sixth graders, and some are now in high school. Here's what they say about the tools, techniques, and processes they use in their work.

As you can tell, these student tutorial designers are proud of their work. The confidence in their answers to my questions speaks volumes about the sense of autonomy, mastery, and purpose this work has instilled in them.

> **Alan:** I want to know about your motivation. I know that designing and creating these presentations is an option and that you guys aren't graded on this work. So, could one of you students explain why you spend such a tremendous amount of time designing these video tutorials?
>
> **Student:** Hi, this is Paul. I personally did them because it helps me understand the math problem better. When you explain it, you're basically reteaching it to yourself so that really helps you understand it. And also, it's really fun. So it's a win-win situation.
>
> **Alan:** Paul, maybe you or one of your friends could explain how you approach designing one of these videos. Do you think of ideas first and then sketch them out? Or do you just start? Do you figure it out as you go? Do you test it out with friends? What's your design process?

continued →

Student: It's basically improv. We look at the math problem we want to do and then we just start, and that's how it goes. If we mess up, we cut out the part that we messed up. We just keep continuing.

Alan: So you just use the editing functions of the software to polish it up at the end.

Student: Yes, it's completely unscripted.

Alan: Do you ever get a response from your peers that gives you ideas for the next one?

Student: This is Jerry. Sometimes I know that a lot of my friends watch the videos, and if they did like something about the video then they usually say, "Oh I liked how you said what this definition is." So sometimes I do get ideas; I do when I make videos.

Alan: So feedback from your friends helps you design the next one sometimes.

Student: Yes.

Alan: What about the idea that your videos are seen around the world, and by college professors and librarians in Australia? Does that have any impact on your sense of accomplishment or motivating to do more?

Student: Hi, this Bob. Yes, knowing that my videos are being shown throughout the United States and more, I guess, just makes you feel special, I guess, that you're helping people not only in your classroom, your school, or even your country, but everywhere.

Alan: Have you had any experience like this in another classroom?

Student: Hi, it's Billy. I'm in tenth grade now, so I'm in chemistry. One of my friends was absent one day when we were learning about dimensional analysis, and it's a really visual process. So I have an old Mac computer with AppleWorks, and I downloaded Jing and made her a video with Jing and AppleWorks. I sent it to her and she got it, and then she understood the topic so it was really great.

Alan: So it's just a nice skill to have.

Student: Yes, it was just so good because it's hard to teach something over the phone and I wanted to show her but I couldn't. Then I sent it to her and she understood it, and it was great.

Alan: What about this idea that students helping students is actually more popular than going to see a teacher after school and asking for extra help? What do you guys think about that?

Student: Hey, it's Bob again. It helps more if students teach students because teachers kind of understand things in their own way. They're just used to knowing everything. But when a student learns it for the first time, it's easier for them to tell another student. I'm not sure if that makes sense the way I'm saying it, but basically students understand students better than they understand teachers.

Alan: In designing one of these tutorials in math, do you remember a time when it helped you understand a concept in a new way or in a deeper way?

Student: Hi, it's Paul again. I know a lot of the time when we were first making the videos in class, Mr. Marcos would teach me something and I would understand it, but not why it would happen. If I asked him he would try to explain it to me, but I just couldn't comprehend. But then, when I would recreate the video, it would all make sense to me because I would have to re-explain it to myself and realize why I was doing everything, as opposed to someone telling me what to do.

Alan: When you had to get up today in front of this audience of teachers and talk about your work, what was that like? How does it feel to be teaching a group of teachers that you have never met before?

Student: It's kind of like making a video almost, because you are talking in front of a bunch of people, and a lot of them don't know your background and some of them do. It's just good to explain what you're doing. I could tell that all of the teachers really appreciated what we did and they all had a really good learning experience. At the end they were all like, "Oh, thank you, this has really affected my teaching methods and everything." (personal communication, October 2011)

Questions for Discussion

1. As an educator, can you name some specific types of lessons or topics that would be particularly well suited for student tutorials?

2. Can you imagine your students creating tutorials (with approval by their teachers) that can help other students learn?

3. How does the work of student tutorial designers fit within Daniel Pink's analysis of purpose as a key motivator of high-quality student work?

4. Beyond the benefits for students who use the tutorials, can you identify educational benefits for students who do the work of tutorial design?

The Student as Scribe

3

In any given class, can you count on all students to take good notes? Do some students struggle in a frantic attempt to record every detail, or seem to draw a blank when identifying the important information in new material? Darren Kuropatwa, a math teacher from McIntyre Collegiate High School in Winnipeg, Manitoba, has developed a solution to this common classroom problem. In his daily scribe model, students produce shared notes. While all the students can take their own notes, the student scribe collects, organizes, and edits a draft of the notes. Darren works with that student to ensure that the details are accurate, and then moves the approved notes to the class blog for use by all students. The Digital Learning Farm job of student scribe follows this same model.

The student scribe work represents low-hanging fruit for educators and students alike. There is very little technology to learn; student scribes can do their work in Google Docs or any of a wide range of online word processing programs, and teachers need only a simple website where they can post the notes for review. Teachers who don't have a class website can even print and distribute hard copies of the notes to the class. In any form, the process of creating and publishing these shared notes offers students a number of benefits. They become better at synthesizing information into ideas, and they learn important skills in collaborating, communicating, organizing, writing, and critical thinking. Best of all, the work can be a lot of fun for the teacher and students alike.

Silvia Tolisano, a 21st century learning specialist at the Martin J. Gottlieb Day School in Jacksonville, Florida, has seen the benefits of leveraging student contributions in the classroom, including the work of official note takers. Silvia's students use Skype to video conference with people in a number of different schools and countries, including subject-area experts who bring valuable insights to class topics. Assigned students work as "back channel" student scribes; they don't participate actively in video conferences. Instead, they remain in the background, noting main topic points in the conference, marking content for editing, and flagging information for fact checking. Of course, Silvia remains responsible for ensuring the accuracy of the notes' content.

When the notes are edited, checked, and ready for online publishing, other class members post the information to the class blog, where it can be accessed and used by anyone—in the classroom or around the world. Working from one set of complete, accurate notes helps everyone focus on the most important information, rather than be distracted by redundancies and the occasional misstatement. The student scribe work also has helped students and staff find even more ways for students to use their skills to make meaningful contributions to their educational experiences. The list of learning jobs continues to grow for this group. "Being able to really tap into their expertise but also their learning style is what developed all of this," Silvia adds. "It just seems normal to allow different students to use different tools." (You will learn more about Silvia Tolisano's use of Digital Learning Farm jobs in the classroom in chapter 5, page 68.)

Brad Ovenell-Carter, head of the THINK Global School, has also incorporated the work of student scribes in his own educational program in a unique way that fits his mobile, multinational school platform. He says, "We have official note takers, one or two students typically. Depending on how complicated the note taking is, we might divide that up between somebody capturing URLs, key dates, or names and spellings, and somebody else taking the general notes. And that's done collaboratively through Google Docs." Brad's students use the comparison of their notes to the official posted version, both as review and reality check: "Other students continue to take their own notes, and then at the end of the class (or maybe two or three classes, depending on how long this little area of interest is going) we put those notes up on the board and sit down as a group, take our personal notes, and ask ourselves, 'Are the notes we've made over the last day or two an accurate reflection of what we talked about?'" That comparison and review helps the class create their official set of notes.

In workshops when introducing the concept of using student scribes to teachers, there are usually some questions about what can go wrong, questions such as:

- What happens to the other students' focus when they know that someone else is responsible for taking the official notes?

- What about the student who can't write well?

- Isn't it unfair to ask that student to publish notes for the whole class to see?

Fortunately, Darren's thoughtful care in building his students' skill sets through this type of in-class contribution provides a model that answers these concerns and more.

In Darren's classes, students who never took notes in the past now work hard to accurately record class content because they know that their work will be published on the class blog, and that their peers depend on the accuracy of the information. Darren also sees students who struggle to take notes get better by studying and using the high-quality work of other students. Darren's pioneering work demonstrates how the use of student scribes can change the dynamic of multiple aspects of the learning experience, including homework, review, and assessment.

The Story: The Student Scribe Program Lifts Learning

Darren Kuropatwa is somewhat of a celebrity among educators. His work with educational blogging has drawn international attention and praise, and his innovative techniques have been an inspiration to me. He has crafted a series of responsibilities for students that results in a wonderful collaboration of work in his classrooms. I asked him once to tell me how he began this process. (A link to this three-part interview can be found at http://novemberlearning .com in the podcasts under Resources.)

He says, "I stumbled on educational blogging over a winter holiday preparing for a workshop I was going to do for other teachers." After presenting the workshop, Darren started his own blog as he was preparing to wrap up his first semester math course. He used the blog to share links to information his class had covered in its coursework. Darren continued the blog over the next semester, but by the summer he began looking for ways to involve his students. "I wanted the blog to be in their voices," he stresses, "not mine."

Eventually, Darren ran across a video created by another teacher who, at the beginning of each class, asked her students to summarize what they had learned in the previous day's work. Then it clicked: "So I said, 'Oh, that's a neat idea. I could have the students reteach what they learned in class with me each day.'" Darren established a daily scribe program for the class blog. The students' assignment was simple: summarize what you learned in class well enough so that an interested learner can keep up with the work, even if he or she is not in the classroom. At the end of each blog post, the student scribe chose his or her replacement for the following day. "That's it," Darren says. "That's the whole assignment." The program took off immediately, leaving Darren amazed at the dynamics he saw unfolding among his students.

Giving Every Student an Opportunity to Shine

With only one student responsible for recording and posting the day's learning, the students immediately understood that they had to be really good at taking notes. Although only one student a day was under the gun to perform, Darren saw the impact on the entire class. On any given day, the student scribe might approach him saying, "Mr. K, do I understand this properly? Did I get this right?" Darren sees how valuable the process of reviewing and refining the notes can be for helping both him and his students know exactly where the class stands in its grasp of class topics. The scribe postings help Darren determine which ideas he needs to revisit and reinforce before moving on.

Darren recalls one incident in which the student scribe came to him after class, saying, "You know, Mr. K, I don't think I understand this well enough to write a scribe post." Darren asked the girl which parts of the topic she felt shaky about, and as she responded, he could see that she had a better grasp of the material than she realized. "I would say that she knew about 90 percent of what happened in the class that day,"

Darren says. He told her to write the whole thing up in the scribe post, including the information she understood *and* the information she didn't quite get. The next day, after reviewing the student's posting with the class, Darren took time to revisit just the small block of information that hadn't been clear to the scribe—a real time saver for him and his class. "In the past," he says, "I'd have a student say to me, 'I don't understand,' and we would start the whole lesson over again from ground zero. So this was really powerful stuff."

Darren's experience has also demonstrated that the blog provides a forum to make it easier for everyone to join in on topic discussions. As he explains on the blog, "Every voice speaks with the same volume, whereas in a classroom, the popular kids or the vocal kids are heard and the quieter kids sometimes fall through the cracks." When a new student (let's call him David) moved to Winnipeg and joined the class, he sat in a far corner of the room and remained quiet. But when David was tapped to be the student scribe, the rest of the class saw the boy's talent shine. "He did an outstanding job," Darren says. "He incorporated pictures and colors in a meaningful way, and he pushed the envelope of what the other kids were doing."

The next day, when the other students saw his notes, they all asked, "Hey, who's David?" After the boy sheepishly identified himself, the other students let him know how impressed they were with his work. "Wow, that was really cool. Can you show me how you did that?" It was magical for Darren to see this boy transformed from being virtually unknown in the classroom to one of its star players—all because of the good work he did in a math class. "The impact that had on the social dynamic of the classroom," he says. "I mean, it was fantastic. You should have seen the boy's eyes light up. Now he's being honored and regarded well by all of his classmates, and they want to learn from him."

Motivating Students With Feedback From a Worldwide Audience

Students seek recognition from both their peers and their teachers. Working as a student scribe brings that recognition to students, along with some valuable sources of meaningful feedback. Darren has found that much of the blog's power with students comes from the fact that its content is viewed by people from around the world. "And I'm deliberate about that too," Darren says. "The blog is open. On the sidebar of the blog we've got a little map, a cluster map that shows every hit that the blog has received from anywhere around the world. If we get a hit, there's a little red dot; more hits from the same locale, and the red dot gets bigger. Over the course of the semester, eventually the map gets obliterated with red dots as people visit our class blog."

Darren believes that the public forum for his students' work plays a big role in the effectiveness of the student scribe program. Think about the typical classroom assignment: students turn in an assignment, the teacher marks it up, and returns it to the students with a grade or number attached. The students look at the assessment and toss it in the trash. They have performed in front of an audience of one, and so the performance is finished. Putting the scribe posts up for class discussion every morning brings peer recognition, but the audience and impact of the program doesn't stop there: "When they're getting recognition from their peers for doing really good academic work, they're motivated to do better. But when you blow the walls off [the classroom], then learning happens anytime, anywhere. Other people see that and they're moved to make a comment [because] the kid did something exemplary. Kids very much think that they are who other people see them as being, and when other people see them as being good in math, then they want to be good in math and they work at being better at it."

To help students get the most benefit from all of this attention, Darren looks for mentors—educators, retired professionals, and other respected readers—who will interact with his students by commenting on their postings. He asks those mentors to comment with what he refers to as "a star and a wish." They might say, for example, "I really like what you did here—great job—but I wish you had kind of explored this in a little more depth." Those kinds of comments push the students to expand their thinking.

Commenters on the blog have included a curriculum designer from Ohio, a professor of mathematics from the University of Michigan, and a teacher who helps other educators introduce new technologies into their classrooms. Darren suggests to these reviewers that "whenever the mood moves them, [they] . . . drop in, look at what the kids are saying, and reply to it." He notes, "I have a large network of colleagues, professionals from all over the world, through Twitter. So I'll tweet out to my network there, saying, 'I'd really appreciate if someone could give this student a push in the right direction or if someone could just check out what this student did. Any praise you leave would be greatly appreciated.'"

The feedback the students get from the readers of their postings is incredibly motivating. Darren tells of one student who was struggling in math, and when it came her time to be the student scribe, she decided to knock the assignment out of the park. The rest of the students in the class had raised the bar with their good work, and she didn't want to fall short. "So she writes this really awesome post and goes on and on with pictures that she has designed by herself. She did it [in] Paint and then embeds these pictures in her post and explains everything. Shortly after that she withdraws from the course. She drops it." A week later, Darren received an email from a colleague in Scotland who said, "Just wanted to give you a heads up. Thought that this particular scribe post was exemplary, and I've just finished showing it off to our national conference of teachers here." The next time Darren saw the girl, he told her about the rave review. "You should have seen the look on her face! Just priceless. Eventually she did come back to class and took the course again, and she did all right." Visit http://thescribepost.pbworks.com/w/page/22148105 /HallOfFame to see some of the best student scribe work from Darren's class.

Building Lifelong Learners and Their Legacy

Just about every educator wants to transform students into lifelong learners. We all know that learning opportunities are never limited to a single time and space, so we have to be prepared to apply our "learner's mind" throughout our lives. Because it enables students to expand the learning experience beyond the space and time traditionally occupied by the classroom and schoolwork, the student scribes approach encourages students to embrace learning as an ongoing, organic experience. And because students can access the blog anytime and from anyplace, they're better able to accommodate their own patterns of behavior within the learning process.

Using collaborative blogging and podcast tools such as Blogger (www.blogger.com), WordPress (www.wordpress.com), wikis, Google Docs (http://docs.google.com), or Zoho Docs (www.zoho.com), educators can expand the learning experience into anytime and anyplace. (Visit **go.solution-tree.com/instruction** for live links to the websites mentioned in this book.) Giving students this extended responsibility for crafting their educational process not only gives them a model for developing the habits of lifelong learners, but it also encourages them to consider the learning legacy they leave for others. Darren sees his students view their work in an entirely new light as a result of their participation as student scribes. They no longer produce work simply for their teachers or parents, and then toss it away once they receive a grade. Now they understand they are creating work that will remain before a worldwide audience long after they leave Darren's class.

Things They Leave Behind

Darren Kuropatwa knows that his students care very much about the legacy their work leaves behind. He is still surprised at the powerful, motivating force of that legacy, though. He says, "I had a kid write a scribe post, just a short paragraph, no pictures, no diagram." Darren showed the piece to some of his fellow educators, and they were unimpressed. Where were the detailed discussions, the animations, or the images that Darren's other students commonly used in their posts? When he explained this student was not a native speaker of English, their responses changed: "They said, 'Well, yeah, actually it's amazing that a non-English-speaking student could produce a paragraph of that length about math, which is like learning a whole other language.'" Darren put the student's work up the next day, as he does with every student scribe blog, and—in his "star and a wish" approach—he told the boy what he liked about the work, then gave him some ideas for how he might have made it better.

A year later, Darren wanted to show the student's work to another teacher, but when he went back to that scribe posting on the blog, he found that the work was changed. In its place was a much longer post that had been formatted differently and included some of the images and ideas that Darren had mentioned in his critique. Why would the student have gone back and edited his work? "There's no way he did it for me," Darren says. "I'm confident that the major motivation for him [was that] he knew other people were going to see it through the years to come." How often do students return to a finished assignment after the semester ends, and continue to improve a piece of work? That can happen when students feel that the work has ongoing purpose.

The power of student legacy has proven to be one of the most surprising benefits of the student scribe program for Darren and his classes. Although people tend to think that digital information is ephemeral, Darren knows that many student works on paper have a much shorter life: "The stuff my kids [handed in to me] five years ago on paper, I gave it back, and I don't know where it is today. I'm pretty sure they don't, either. [But] the digital stuff my kids did five years ago, it's still there, and it will probably still be there when their grandchildren want to see it."

That's not to say that every incoming class can simply skip the learning process and re-create the scribe blogs from years past. In fact, Darren makes sure the students in each class understand that they are writing their own textbook and that their experience will be unique, just as it was for every class that came before them. Darren explains, "I'm not the same person a year later. My understanding of the material and the pedagogy gets better incrementally year to year. So the way I deliver that content is changing, and I'm trying to do a better job at it. Also, the student whose turn it is to write the scribe post is [unique]. Every scribe, therefore, has to write their own page in the class's learning record, and each leaves his or her own legacy."

Tools and Techniques: Adopting the Student Scribes Approach

So what do teachers need to know in order to pull off the same kind of success Darren Kuropatwa achieved with student scribes in the classrooms? According to Darren, adopting this kind of program involves a shift in control and pedagogy, as well as an openness to imagine the possibilities offered by available technologies. However, perhaps the biggest challenges for some teachers will be redefining the role of the learner as contributor, and building a collaborative learning culture.

Although an increasing number of educators are comfortable with a wide range of digital tools, others aren't. As Darren says, "Sometimes they just need to see an example and let that percolate—but that's just the beginning. Then the main thing is to get past the fear (of losing control)." Darren speaks of one teacher who was doing really good work with his students, publishing their notes on a wiki along with his daily lesson plans and other student work. But he wouldn't open the wiki up to readers outside his class. When Darren asked him why he wouldn't let others read the work, the teacher said, "Who cares? Who wants to see my stuff? It's not that good." Darren explains that every example of this kind of student scribe work and class blogging serves as a valuable model for others who are considering starting a similar program in their own classes. "I don't know why a lot of my colleagues just have this reluctance to think that they can be really good at what they do," Darren says, adding that it's also important to share mistakes that are made. He says, "As long as you're willing to put yourself out there and share, you get back many fold over what you give."

Anyone who can send an email can use the technologies necessary to launch a class blog, wiki, and student scribe program. Writing with a blog post editor in WordPress or other blogging software looks and feels much like writing an email message. First efforts might seem humble, but the work grows easier and more effective over time. As Darren explains, "Don't look at my blogs today and say, 'That's where I need to be tomorrow,' because it's taken me years to get here." And remember, most educators will find that their students will master the process more quickly than they will. Class blogs and online textbooks get even better when the students begin to innovate and take the site designs and capabilities to the next level. That kind of pushback helps everyone in the class (including the teacher) get better at his or her online work.

Educators can tap their students' technical savvy and increase class ownership in the learning process by asking students to help teach each other how to do specific tasks (such as embedding images, filming video, and so on). Darren sees that "the kids realize that it's really all about them working together as a community, and they begin to lean on each other to be successful in their learning. It's not about any one of them. It's about all of them pulling together. I work very hard on that piece in class, and that's pedagogy. That has nothing to do with technology."

Darren Kuropatwa's students, in essence, *author* their course textbook, a technique that other teachers have begun to adopt. That level of involvement has implications for everyone in the classroom. "I expect these kids every day to write something significant and meaningful about what they learned," Darren notes, "so I'd better deliver and give them stuff that they can articulate. If you can push the kids or if you can evolve your class to the point where it feels like a learning community where every kid is dependent upon every other kid for their learning and they feel this reliance on each other, then good things happen. And you don't have to be the expert who knows all these technical details. The kids can do that." Darren recommends that teachers begin by spending a half day or so of class time going over the specific type of collaborative tool the students will use in the student scribe process. That time can involve going over the goals for the scribe posts, outlining how to set up the blogging or other program, reviewing the basic option settings, and then, as Darren says, "You're off to the races."

 On his professional blog (http://adifference.blogspot.com), Darren documents his step-by-step development of the class blog, the scribe post phenomenon, and how the whole process unfolded with his classes. People from around the globe visit his site, and Darren receives emails from many educators who tell him they are implementing similar programs in their own classes. Darren is amazed at the variety of their efforts: "I've seen it in science classes, I've seen it in religion classes; I've seen it in ELA classes from grade 5 through grade 12. I've even had conversations with teachers about how you might do something similar with even younger kids. Little kids can document what they've learned, maybe with a digital camera and then using something like VoiceThread, that they can articulate what we're looking at in the picture. There are lots of ways that students can share what they know." (VoiceThread is a free collaborative tool that enables users to create and view slideshows of images, documents, and videos. Viewers can add comments to the VoiceThread show in five different forms, including spoken comments. Go to http://voicethread.com for more details.)

Educators can expect to stumble occasionally as they begin weaving the use of digital tools into their pedagogies. Darren advises newcomers to the student scribe program to look at the work of others who are early in the process of adopting this model: "Teachers who are far along in the adoption curve . . . can certainly be models and resources. [But] I think the best models we have for teachers are other teachers at the early part of the adoption curve." Darren's point that early adopters can be helpful to newbies is very important. Recent adopters are closest to the experience of teachers who are just beginning to rethink the culture of their classrooms.

As I've listened to Darren speak of his experiences over the years, I've come to realize that the real boundary he is asking people to jump over in making the leap to this educational approach isn't a technical boundary; it's a "shift of control" boundary. He went through that shift stage by stage as he asked his students to take on more shared learning responsibilities. I asked him once if he thought that his level of expertise had begun to create a distance between him and less technically adept educators. In fact, the process seems to have connected him to a broader group of teachers at all levels of technical expertise.

"It's funny," he says. "I started blogging with my students and, as I said earlier, it was mostly my voice. I saw the blog as a place to pull in resources from the Internet, aggregate them in one place, and share them with my class. Eventually, I felt the need to talk to other teachers (and not my students) online to get that feedback from a larger community. That pushed me to get my own blog, and through the interaction with other teachers on my own blog it shifted and changed what I did on my class blog."

Darren encourages teachers simply to start the scribes program and class blog or wiki, and to view it as something that they do with their classes. Then the project can grow organically along with the teacher's and class's experience. "If you found some neat resources at a conference or if someone shared a useful link with you or you found a video on YouTube you thought was really instructive," Darren advises, "then just start a blog where you aggregate that stuff. I've seen a lot of teachers kind of use what I think of as homework blogs. They just kind of announce, 'This is tonight's homework, and this assignment is due tomorrow.'" Again, it's best to start out slowly and simply, and let the work grow along with the users' confidence.

At the same time, Darren urges teachers to continue to push themselves: "As long as you're asking what's next, you'll get there. But never be content with where you're at." While collaborating with other educators can also help teachers develop their use of educational blogs and student scribes, many find that others in their school system simply aren't interested. In that case, as Darren advises, use your online resources: "That's where something like Twitter or any type of professional learning network becomes really valuable."

Teachers can also network with other educators who are using the student scribe model and other new learning models through professional online social websites. Ning, an online platform for creating social websites, hosts one dedicated to professional educator development, called the Educator's Professional Learning Network Ning (or the Educator's PLN Ning). Visit www.ning .com for a free thirty-day trial. The Educator's PLN is at http:// edupln.ning.com. Also, http://englishcompanion.ning.com is offered for English teachers, and http://isenet.ning.com is offered for independent school teachers.

The information and exchange of ideas on such a site can be invaluable to any educator. As Darren notes, "Even if all you do is lurk and listen to what other people are talking about, maybe that's a way to start. [Listen] to what other people are doing and say, 'Oh, I think I can try that and just do one thing, one thing a month, or one thing in two months, and see what happens.'"

Questions for Discussion

1. What do you see as the potential benefits and downsides to incorporating the work of student scribe into your classes?

2. What benefits do you see for students who publish to a global audience?

3. Do you think students will work harder on material that they prepare for that audience than they will when doing work for their teachers?

4. How can teachers model sharing knowledge with a global audience?

The Student as Researcher

What if that unused computer at the back of the classroom became the official research station where one student each day was responsible for finding answers to questions in class—including the teacher's questions? What if students were better trained to vet the information they find so their research could be more useful to them and to the entire class? All of these outcomes are possible when we incorporate the job of student researcher into our educational model. Let me tell you about an experience that helped me understand the important implications for this role in the Digital Learning Farm.

I was once invited to visit a middle school that was in the same quaint seaside Cape Cod community as the Woods Hole Oceanographic Institute. While I was working with Woods Hole scientists to organize a climate change conference for teachers, I was asked if I would visit the middle school to speak with one of its classes about climate change. When I reached the school, I was ushered into a computer lab filled with eager and very polite middle school students. What happened next caused me to rethink how we prepare our students to research the web.

I began my presentation by explaining to students that Woods Hole scientists were predicting a rise in ocean levels as the climate warmed on our planet. Immediately a hand shot up. "Where will the new beach be if the ocean rises?"

The student who had asked the question was sitting in front of me with a laptop. In what I would like to think was a nice supportive response, I said something like, "I bet you can find the answer yourself with your laptop. There are interactive maps online that will let you type in a number of feet of sea rise and zoom in on any part of the world to see the impact of sea water flooding." At first the student hesitated, and then he got to work. I had to give him some further assistance, but in a few minutes he was typing numbers into a website and watching the seacoast being redrawn. "Whoa!" he yelped.

A girl next to him could see how excited he was about discovering his own answer. In what can only be described as an apologetic voice, and without telling me what her question was, she asked, "May I answer my own question, too?" I was a bit stunned that she felt she had to ask my permission to find her own answer. I nodded, and the girl immediately began searching online for information about issues that contribute to climate change. As if a dam had broken loose, soon nearly every student in the class was on a mission to track down information about climate change.

After a while, I asked the students if they would design a search that would only yield results from Iceland about the impact of climate change on the melting glaciers. None of them could do it—but they all thought they could. Every student was using Google, a search tool that they all felt fully versed in using. I could clearly see, however, that they didn't know how Google ranked results, nor did they understand the concept of country codes or how to use the search engine's Advanced Search button to limit their results to one part of the world. Most importantly, they did not understand why they had failed. Clearly, none of these students, in spite of his or her readily available online access, had been taught how to conduct an accurate search. I left the school that day worried that we have not truly defined what we mean by web literacy or how it should be taught.

For example, we can't assume that if students can read and write, they can search the web. The web has its own very specific architecture of information that is quite different than the way we typically organize information on paper. The web also has its own grammar, punctuation, and syntax, as well as its own rules for storing and retrieving information. The students I met that day were using paper literacy skills to navigate in a digital world, and coming up with misleading and shallow results.

There are so many nuances to searching the web and so many search tools that can aid that process:

- Twitter's search engine (http://twitter.com/search)
- Google's Advanced Search tools (www.google.com/advanced_search)
- WolframtAlpha, the knowledge engine (www.wolframalpha.com)
- Diigo, the social bookmarking site (www.diigo.com)

With all of these online searching aids at our disposal, we should be committing to teaching our children accurate and creative searching techniques that are applicable across every discipline. One way to structure this learning experience for children and educators is through the use of student researchers.

This student work might not sound particularly exciting or imaginative. And, yes, I understand that teaching students how to conduct accurate online searches and other types of data-gathering activities does not fully school them in the techniques of classical scientific research. At the same time, making students the researchers can bring real benefits to both the teaching *and* learning experiences. It can engage students in the learning process, improve their use of search tools, and make them savvier information analysts by teaching them how to vet sources for reliability. Student researchers learn to ask better questions, find real answers, and apply the information they uncover in their work.

With most students (and many professionals) relying almost exclusively on the Internet for research, and with facts fighting for space among the misinformation that floods the web, these skills are critical. In this chapter, we'll take a closer look at the work of the student researcher, the ways some educators have incorporated that work into their students' activities, and the tools and techniques teachers have used to gain full value from this important form of student contribution.

The Story: Student Researchers Develop Critical Skills

Many teachers who have seen students turn in shallow (or worse, plagiarized) academic work with data gleaned from only the top screen of online search results understandably have a hard time believing students will be willing to invest the time, intellect, energy, and persistence necessary to do accurate online searches. Fortunately, we can look to a number of pioneers who are leading the way in training and using student researchers to bring real value to their work—both in the classroom and outside it.

One of the most astonishing gaps in many students' educations is their inability to validate information on the Internet. And this is the generation many refer to as "digital natives"? Well, they may have been born after the web was invented, but that has nothing to do with their understanding of the architecture of information on the Internet. In fact, many students who use the Internet on a daily basis remain web-illiterate. Furthermore, you cannot assume that because your students seem comfortable around digital devices, they are knowledgeable about critical thinking.

Even when students are trained to become web-literate in one course or in the library, they often don't transfer these skills to other courses and settings. Just as we do with reading and writing, if we are to truly educate our children to think critically on the web, we must train them to apply the same rigor and discipline to their online research that they apply to other skills across the curriculum.

My own "aha" moment about the importance of teaching students rigorous online searching skills came in the mid-1990s, compliments of a fourteen-year-old student named Zack, who researched and wrote a history paper about "how the Holocaust never happened." When I asked Zack where he'd gathered his information, he said he found it on a website at Northwestern University with the address (http://pubweb .northwestern.edu/~abutz/di/intro.html). He was right; a Northwestern professor named Arthur Butz had posted his own website at that address, through the university's domain. In it, Butz matter-of-factly explained the inaccuracies within what he described as the "erroneous belief" in the "legend" of the Holocaust.

Putting aside the site's list of improbable alternative explanations for everything—from the gas chambers to the death rates found within the concentration camps—try to imagine how a fourteen-year-old boy might have viewed the reliability of this information. The content wasn't laced with the fire-breathing rhetoric of hatred, and it was written by a professor at Northwestern University. To this boy, who knew that Northwestern was an important university, this information had to be true!

If Zack would have been trained in how to interpret the address of this site, he would have known that it linked to a personal webpage, rather than to an official site of Northwestern University. That fact was evident in the pubweb designation at the address's beginning and the tilde sign that preceded the author's abbreviated name within the address. In other words, this site's address revealed that it was simply the personal posting of an employee of the university, not an official document offered *by* Northwestern University. (Later we will return to Zack's example and the specific techniques for teaching students to assess the origin of information.)

That page has long since disappeared from the Northwestern site (you can quickly retrieve it by typing the web address into the Wayback Machine at www.archive.org), but I'm afraid that inadequate training in Internet searching remains in too many classrooms. Clearly, the Internet has become a dominant medium for information in our society and our students must be trained in how to validate the content they find there. Essentially, all serious commentary about educating students in 21st century skills includes ideas and concerns about online literacy. Students must learn how to research, publish, and communicate through and with the Internet and other information tools. By training and using students as researchers, we can give our kids the fundamental skills they need to begin handling these tasks. That training has to include techniques for applying knowledge to produce information and facili-tate communication, and one of the most important skills in that task will involve evaluating the resources they decide to use. Visit http://novemberlearning.com/resources/information-literacy-resources/ for support with learning web literacy.

When educators begin incorporating the work of student researcher into their classroom programs, the school librarian can become a vital source of guidance for the students' work. Joyce Valenza is the librarian at Springfield Township High School in Pennsylvania. In a conversation published on my website, she discusses the importance of librarians in the process of teaching students how to find, validate, and ethically use online information. (Visit http://blog.schoollibraryjournal.com/neverendingsearch/2011/10/04/truth-lies-and-the-internet/ to access Joyce's blog .) Information technology is a big part of every librar-ian's work, and Joyce has developed some very effective ways for educating students in the use of information—in any form.

Joyce understands that changes in the information landscape bring changes to the work of research. She notes, "For learners to become successful in academics and business, they need fluencies that they didn't used to need, including how to find, use, and communicate information. I want my students to leave my library able to produce factual and ethical information, to use video to explore ideas, and to use the Internet and collaborative tools for research" (personal communication, November 2011).

As we all know, the numbers and natures of those tools have expanded incredibly in the 21st century.

Take, for example, the topic of wikis—crowd-sourced collections of information that can be as large as the online encyclopedia Wikipedia, or as small as a class wiki that offers student tutorials and notes. As Joyce has seen, many educators dismiss the entire idea of using wikis because they aren't validated sources of information. But since many basic searches return results from Wikipedia or other "unofficial" sources, how are students to understand when and how wiki information can play a valid role in research?

"If you have already put Wikipedia in a box [that labels it 'bad'] and refuse to reconsider it, you don't know about it and can't use it in any form," Joyce says, "but at the same time, how are you going to teach students to have the flexibility they need to succeed if you don't demonstrate that flexibility yourself?" As Joyce explains, if a student is searching for information about elements of pop culture, Wikipedia may be a logical place to look. "For instance, if I am researching the history of Superman, my visit to Britannica or any of those traditional sources will be quite limited because they don't concern themselves that much with popular information and they're not [necessarily] accessing the experts on Superman. On Wikipedia, those Superman people are going crazy collecting [information on] everything from the first comic book to the last movie, lists of characters, and details about their superpowers." She adds, "The *American Idol* site itself is less rich than the Wikipedia site about *American Idol*." (Britannica stopped printing its book edition with the 2010 edition. This was announced in March of 2012.)

Fast-moving current events are sometimes given the earliest documentation by Wikipedia contributors and other "feet on the street" people, not by official news sources. "When the London bombings in 2005 were happening," Joyce says, "people contributed information to Wikipedia about it that the BBC couldn't keep up with." The multiple Arab Spring uprisings in 2011 offer another example of unfolding events that were first reported and recorded by Twitter and Facebook users, rather than by official news sources.

At the same time, data-gathering students have to understand what not to look for on group-sourced sites. "If I'm looking for scholarly criticism about Macbeth," she explains, "I won't look at Wikipedia. I teach my high school students that scholars aren't being rewarded for publishing on the site, so that's not where they put their greatest energy. As a hobbyist, they might visit, but they won't spend hours correcting the material they find there."

In other words, Joyce works to train student researchers to understand when, why, and how to use online content. By training students in these tasks, she teaches them to understand how to evaluate the information they find so they understand where it fits in what Joyce calls their "research toolkit." To do that, Joyce asks the student researchers she works with to consider a series of questions: "What is your information path? What is your information need? Who is discussing your information?" Further, Joyce encourages students to think about what type of information sources their teacher (or their boss, supervisor, or other audience) prefer and respect. Then, students can consider all of those conditions when evaluating their sources.

Joyce also encourages educators to guide student researchers to explore beyond common wisdom when gathering information. Most major news sites repeat the same Associated Press news releases, for example, but if students want to gain fresh insights, they need to gather multiple perspectives. "We need to teach people that they aren't always looking for the biggest curve that information takes," she says, "but [rather] the smaller aspects that can get dropped from major sources." In other words, the work of the student researcher involves building a larger researcher's toolkit and at the same time developing both the understanding and the flexibility necessary to use it well.

Joyce has learned how to tackle some of the hurdles to adapting research to new types of information sources and technologies. As she explains, "For instance, for equity issues, I need a page on my site to lead students to open-source materials so every student can do a presentation on a word processing document, even if they don't have the software." By linking students to free downloadable resources, Joyce eliminates one of the largest barriers to publishing student research findings.

At the same time, Joyce leads student researchers to materials that enable them to publish and broadcast their findings ethically, with respect for intellectual property rights. Joyce has created pages that lead them to materials that are part of creative common licensing. That includes photos, open-source video tools, image databases that are copyright friendly, government databases, and so on. In the process, students (and teachers) learn more about Creative Commons licensing.

Joyce also works to lead student researchers to educational streaming media that brings in news and other resources from foreign countries "so students can get practice listening to news from original sources and perspectives from around the world." Joyce sees her role as a school librarian intimately linked to the role of data gathering and synthesis for student researchers: "I want to gather primary source documents. I want to help students access sites, to collect eBooks and wiki books."

In all of her efforts, Joyce demonstrates her commitment to teaching students the best way to access, evaluate, and use data. And she stresses that every educator must realize that his or her approach to teaching research techniques must evolve right along with the widely available information sources. "It's no longer enough to have a physical library with an online catalog," she argues. "If you're not pulling in the resources that those students need to look at, you're not really a 21st century librarian."

Blogging the Research Process

Beginning back in 2004, Joyce encouraged the student researchers in her school to blog about their major research findings and process. According to her blog, "In our school, Pennsylvania's traditional senior project involves an outside mentored experience, a major research paper, a project resulting from the experience and the research, and a presentation of the semester-long exploration. A project like this cries out to be blogged!"

Joyce also offers five reasons why student researchers should blog about their experiences. First, blogging about their research processes helps them reflect on the successes and weaknesses in that work, and how they might improve the process in future work. Second, blogging helps student researchers organize their processes and outline their steps, important for any published results. At the same time, the blog enables the researchers and readers to spot and correct gaps, define terms, and so on. Third, the blog allows others to follow along, to learn from the successes and mistakes of the blogging researcher. Fourth, by offering processes, findings, and links, the blogs create pathways to information that other researchers can use in their work. And, finally, blogging helps spark interactions that can benefit both the blogging student researcher and his or her readers. Educators can follow student researcher blogs to guide and coach the kids in their work. In fact, anyone who reads the blog (including other students and mentors) can add his or her own words of advice and support.

Tools and Techniques: Guiding Student Researchers

The work of the student researcher can be quite straightforward. Consider an example offered by Brad Ovenell-Carter, head of the THINK Global School (an alternative school with no fixed buildings, address, or even nationality). Although the THINK Global School is a highly unusual educational program, the work that Brad and his team are doing offers an exciting example of the way 21st century educators are preparing students to succeed in today's global society. Brad fully understands the potential uses and benefits of the work of student researcher. Each day, one of the school's teachers might assign a different student to work at the class computer. When questions come up during class, that student is responsible for searching out the correct answer. When the student researcher finds that information (from a reliable source), the student shares it with the class. Even better, the class researchers can add the sites they find and approve to a customized search engine for the use of the entire class, and for those classes that follow. You can learn how to design and use your own custom search engine; visit www. google.com/cse for basic how-to information.

All of that requires some basic skills for finding, vetting, and publishing information. Let's explore some of the tools and techniques educators can use to bring these skills to the work of student researchers in their own classrooms.

Assessing Online Information Sources

Remember Zack and his "Holocaust denial" report? How could Zack—or any student—have determined that Professor Butz's website contained personal opinion, rather than official documentation from Northwestern University? I believe that educators need to tell their student researchers to examine any information in terms of three aspects: purpose, author, and place. For online information, I often refer to this last category as metaweb information, and by that, I am referring to the information's relationship to the rest of the web as determined by its address, links, and other sites that link to it.

The first task becomes teaching students to determine exactly what the information is trying to accomplish. If the site was created to sell or promote a product or service, its purpose is relatively clear. Students need to look at commercial sites as sales tools first, with the information they offer as part of the toolkit. The purpose of noncommercial sites can be more difficult to pin down. Is the site advocating some issue or idea? Making this assessment teaches students to look beyond the surface of any information or idea to understand its context and, more precisely, identify its mission.

A website's purpose will not always be clear. Professor Butz's site is a great example; it appeared to be an objective fact sheet of information, but it was most certainly advocating Holocaust denial. We cannot anticipate every hidden message our students might encounter online, so we have to make sure they understand how to examine all information in order to determine its purpose. The first step in that process is knowing that purpose might not be obvious.

The next step student researchers must take in testing the validity of online information is to examine its author. Anyone can sound like an expert, but not everyone has a background that would support that label. I recommend that we teach our students to run searches on the sources of online information in order to see what else those sources have published, as well as their personal and professional backgrounds. If Zack had run a search on Arthur Butz and discovered that his writings were flagged as anti-Semitic by hatewatch.org and listed as important "re-education" material by whitepower.org, he might have realized that the professor's work had a very clear agenda.

Finally, we can teach students to examine the "place" of online information by studying the information's context in terms of other web information. Students should know that information from a personal home page, for example, holds a different context and use for purposes of research than information from an educational institution or government site. Website domain names contain this information as:

- **.com**—a commercial or for-profit organization
- **.org**—a nonprofit organization designation (that anyone can apply for)
- **.net**—a public or private network
- **.gov**—a government agency
- **.K12**—a school

As mentioned earlier, the tilde within a URL is a clear indicator that the site is a personal website. Knowing that, Zack would have understood that the information on Arthur Butz's site was posted on his personal website and not an official posting of his work at the university. Teachers can ask their students to examine a variety of site domain names to determine what type of organization is offering the site, and discuss with the class what types of research might make use of information from each of these types.

Next, we can teach our students how to understand how a website is linked to other information on the Internet. The link: command is one of many strategies for revealing this information. When you are on a website, you can click on its outgoing links to see what other sites it links to. Unless you use the link: command, however, you cannot see which websites are linking *into* the website you are visiting. Why does this information matter? Because it enables you to see how other sites are referencing the site and commenting on its content.

For example, if you run a specialized search in Google (typing in the command *link:www.martinlutherking.org*) you will see hundreds of sites that have linked into that site. Many of these incoming links originate at university libraries, which explain on their sites that even though the www.martinlutherking.org site appears to provide educational material for students to understand Martin Luther King Jr., it is owned by a white supremacy group. Without running the link: command, you might not ever be aware of the academic community's commentary about the site. By teaching our students this and similar "smartsearch" techniques, we provide them with essential tools and strategies for validating information from the web. See http://novemberlearning.com for more strategies educators can use to help their students become more web literate.

Because children at very young ages are learning to search for and access online information, teaching them how to assess the validity of that material is an essential task for educators today. By incorporating the work of student researcher in the educational program, we provide a perfect platform for teaching and practicing this important skill set.

Building a Custom Search Engine

Kids who know how to use a search engine should also know how to build one. Why? First, it gives students a deeper understanding of how a search engine works, which improves their ability to conduct more productive searches. More directly, however, building a custom search engine that references content relevant to grade level, community, course content, and research topics gives students vital practice in working with online information. It also provides a marvelous vehicle for collaborating with other students and topic experts from within your school and across the globe. This kind of collaboration results in a search engine that represents a student legacy, a tool that other students can use in the years ahead.

With a Google account, students can use Google Custom Search (www.google .com/cse/) to build a search engine designed to search a specific set of sites. Students can make the search engine available anytime, from anyplace, by putting a link to it within their blog, wiki, or class home page. As the creators of the search engine, students control the types of sites it searches. So, for example, a class studying America's history of manned space flight could limit searches to NASA and other official scientific aeronautical research sites, rather than including UFO blogs, moon-landing conspiracy theorists, and other less-relevant types of information sources.

Visit http://tinyurl.com/2e25qz to see the custom search engine, Expanding Your Horizons. You can also visit www.customsearchengine.com/index.php?list=top to access the Google directory of custom search engines at. (Visit **go.solution-tree .com/instruction** for live links to the websites mentioned in this book.) When you click on any custom search engine page, you will see introductory text that explains the purpose of the site and some of the resources it includes in its searches. The page also enables users to link the custom search engine to their own home pages, blogs, or search engines. See figure 4.1 for an example of a link directory containing several custom Google search engines.

Figure 4.1: This link directory lists a number of Google custom search engines.
Source: Polite, 2011. Used with permission.

Building the customized search engine is easy. Visit www.google.com to sign up for a Google account. Afterward, when you sign in to Google, you will see your email address showing at the top of the Google page. Check out www.youtube.com/watch?v=IeiFFpo8qME for a YouTube video that explains how to design a custom search engine.

With your account in order, return to the custom search page located at www .google.com/cse/, and click the Create a Custom Search Engine button. After you enter an email address and your Google account password, you can follow the simple on-screen instructions to create the search engine. The instructions page includes an option for testing your search engine before clicking the link to your search engine page. Every search engine you create will be stored on that page. You can access your search engine by clicking the home page link next to its listing. (Visit **go.solution -tree.com/instruction** for live links to the websites mentioned in this book.)

You can share your search engine with others by copying the home page link address to your website (making it available to everyone who accesses your site), or by sending it to individuals in an email message. You can post the search engine link to your blog by clicking the Add This Search Engine to Your Blog or Webpage link at the bottom of the search page. After customizing the appearance of your search engine, click the Get the Code button to receive the HTML code that you can embed in your site to provide search engine access. By doing so, you allow readers to use your custom search engine directly from your blog or website, without entering a lengthy URL. Check out *Web Literacy for Educators* (November, 2008) for more details about these processes.

As you collaborate with others on developing your custom search engine, you can enable others to contribute directly to its list of sites. To do that, go to the search engine control panel and click the Collaboration link. Google takes you to a site that enables you to send invitations to the people that you want to permit to add sites to the search engine. Only the people you designate there will be able to add sites to your search engine. If you want to create a true wiki site that accepts new content from any source, click the Basics link in the control panel.

The web can be overwhelming, and the flood of information it offers can confuse young researchers and complicate their work. By using the techniques outlined here, you can create a search engine that directs students to the type of content that is appropriate for the work they are doing in your classroom, school, or community. The search engine is easy to use and can be an asset in teaching and learning about online research. And remember: if you do create a custom search engine for your students, it will still be important to teach them disciplined research techniques in major search engines like Google.

Is It Cheating? Or Is It Resourceful Research?

Students can become savvy researchers, but sometimes those skills can introduce unexpected issues for educators. Discussing the ethics of using online material gives student researchers and their teachers an opportunity to explore the sometimes fuzzy line that separates "cheating" from "being resourceful."

Here's an example. An eighth-grade student was accessing a social studies website created by a teacher from another school in another state. For some reason, this out-of-state teacher posted the full teacher resources provided by the company that produced the class's textbook,

continued →

including tests, quizzes, and study guides for the course material. When the eighth-grade student's teacher found out he had an advance copy of the quiz she was giving that day, she sent him to the principal.

The student told the principal he had been accessing that type of material all semester by visiting the out-of-state teacher's website, where it was posted for anyone to read. He said he had used the quizzes and tests posted there to study for the same assessments in his own class.

We can probably all agree that the out-of-state teacher shouldn't have posted tests and other assessment tools on a website that was open to all visitors (including the students who were taking the tests). At the same time, many may feel that all teachers should customize their assessments to better reflect their own class's coverage of course material. But the true ethical dilemma here is directed at the student. Was he cheating? What was his crime?

As with many issues involving the use of online material, responsible arguments can be made on both sides. This student was a savvy online researcher; in searching for online content relevant to his course work, he stumbled upon the out-of-state teacher's site and the gold mine of test information it contained. But that information was freely available to all interested readers. It was posted by a teacher. It gave him a very specific study guide, but it didn't negate the kid's need to learn the material. Yes, perhaps he should have told his teacher that he'd found the material, but would we label the student a cheater if his own teacher had handed out the resource material for study?

These are the kinds of questions you could expect to arise in discussing this situation with students and other educators. The process of examining these issues offers everyone an important tool for expanding our understanding of the uses of the millions of resources on the Internet and the information they offer.

Using Advanced Searches

Michael Gorman is an award-winning educator and leader of the Integrated Solutions Block, an educational program that integrates technology with core educational standards at Woodside Middle School near Fort Wayne, Indiana. Michael often speaks about the importance of guiding students in the use of digital technology, and he is particularly passionate on the topic of teaching students to use digital tools more productively. In an important post to my educational blog, Michael outlined some compelling reasons to teach students how to conduct more useful and precise online

searches using one of the most common digital tools, the Google search engine. You can read the full post, "Twelve Reasons to Teach Searching Techniques With Google Advanced Search . . . Even Before Using the Basic Search," at http://novemberlearning.com (Gorman, 2011b).

Michael encourages educators to teach students to use Google's Advanced Search feature, even before they discuss the basic search process with the class. The Advanced Search feature gives users an opportunity to search the Internet for sites and documents containing a collection of specific words, a specific phrase, exact wording, or alternate words (this *or* that). The feature also includes an option for eliminating search results that contain specific words. Users can access Google's Advanced Search feature by clicking the Advanced Search button on the Google page (www.google.com/advanced_search). See figure 4.2 for a screenshot of the Advanced Search feature.

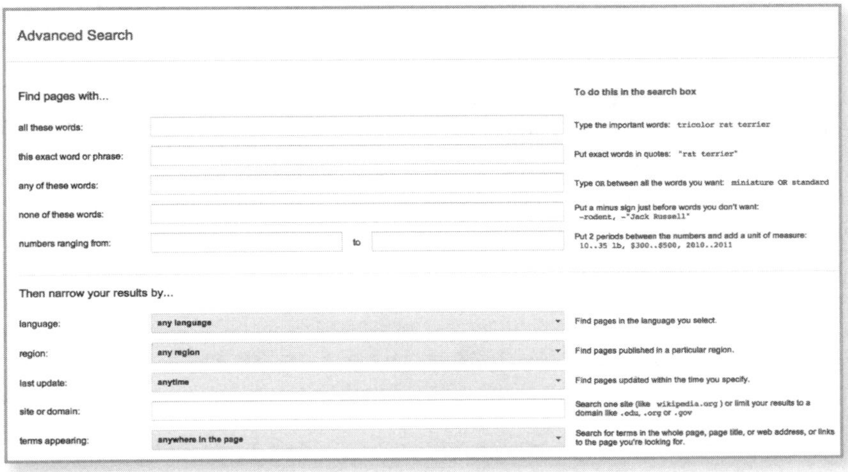

Figure 4.2: Google's Advanced Search feature lets students hone their searches and their search skills.

As Michael notes, Google's Advanced Search feature teaches users the function of important search tools, such as AND statements (through the All These Words option), OR commands (through the One or More of These Words option), NOT statements (through the But Don't Show Pages That Have . . . option) and STRINGs (the This Exact Wording or Phrase option). Tip links on the Advanced Search page help teach users how to use the options in basic searches, as well, and the page also shows users how they would structure the text for a basic version of the same search. Together, this information can teach students the most productive ways to structure their online searches so they get the most accurately targeted results.

Michael also points out another learning bonus available through Google's Advanced Search feature—the option to produce results in any language. "What an awesome way for students to explore a foreign language they are studying or to get primary sources on an event from the source country," he comments. Students also have the option of limiting their searches to a specific website or domain, for example, to find only those results offered by an official government or educational source.

In discussing these and other educational benefits of teaching student researchers to use the Advanced Search tools, Michael stresses that we should teach students to use these tools even when conducting basic searches. "I do not see these skills as advanced techniques," he explains. "I see them as a skill set necessary in finding information in a productive manner. When educators ask students to search and find information on the Internet . . . it is not to just get the answer. It is to learn an important process that will serve them through future schooling and eventual careers." Michael closes his advice on the Google Advanced Search feature by reminding us that teaching students to use its tools correctly will expand our students' digital abilities while making our classrooms even more productive—and it's up to educators to make that happen.

The ideas you've learned here are just some of the tools and techniques available to educators engaged in the critical work of teaching their students to become more savvy and successful users of online information. However you approach the process of training your students in the work of student researcher, make no mistake about its critical importance in their overall education. *If we only teach one skill to prepare our students to survive in a web-based world, it should be that of critical thinking in the analysis of online information.*

Learning the Grammar of Online Search Engines

One of my concerns as I watch students conduct searches is that they don't understand that essentially "no one is home at Google." Search results are generated by an algorithm that does not read English. It is essential that we teach our students the grammar, syntax, and punctuation of the most commonly used source of research.

When I'm working with teachers to teach critical-thinking skills on the web, I use examples to which adults can relate. For example, a teacher in the audience once asked me if I could help her design a search for the most recent research for breast cancer. She told me a friend of hers had recently been diagnosed, and her doctor told her not to go to the web because she would find outdated (and perhaps even bogus) information. Her friend respected her doctor but wanted to take some control over her own choices for treatment, and wanted to become an advocate for her own wellness.

When I challenge an audience to design the search this patient wants, it is common to see the majority type in *recent research* and *breast cancer*. As you might imagine, this is not a good way to start. The search engine is not smart enough to interpret the word *recent*. If there is recent research and the text does not mention the word *recent*, you will not find the content. Similarly, if there is a 2001 article that mentions recent research, you might find it. Also, there is no control over the variety or the quality of the content. A much better way to design the search is to type in *site:gov* or *site:edu* and *breast cancer,* and then use the timeline tool in Google to ensure that your results were posted in the last six months. The site: command allows you to limit your search to one extension (in this case, only government sites or university sites).

In chapter 5, we examine another type of critical student work you can incorporate in the Digital Learning Farm model, that of global communicator and collaborator.

Questions for Discussion

1. If you currently head up a classroom, what is your assessment of your students' abilities to design basic and advanced searches?

2. Do you believe students should be taught to understand search strategies within the context of each discipline?

3. What difficulties do you foresee in assigning the role of student researcher in your classroom? What benefits do you think this work might bring to your students?

4. What if you had to design an assessment item in your content area where your students would have access to the web while they take the test? What would that assessment item look like? How would the question have to differ from one based on memorization?

The Student as Global Communicator and Collaborator

5

In a continuous effort to help my adult children find ways to market themselves to potential employers, I often ask my corporate clients, "What do you value? What are the most important skills you look for in your employees?" When working in London for one of the largest banks in the world, I asked the CEO this question, and he gave me his answer in one word: "Empathy." He went on to say that his company invests in very complicated, very expensive projects, some involving hundreds of people from many different countries, and involving billions of dollars. "To manage complex projects like these, we need people who can understand other points of view," the CEO explained. He added that, in his experience, Europeans are good at valuing multiple perspectives, Africans are pretty good at it, too, and the Chinese are improving. How does the United States fare in this ranking? The CEO told me, "Americans are often inexperienced in valuing other culture's perspectives. Top global talent must understand and value other peoples' points of view. Unfortunately, a lot of Americans think, 'If the world doesn't look like us, it's broken.'"

That CEO isn't alone in his high value of a global perspective. Michael Wesch is a cultural anthropologist, researcher of youth culture on the web, winner of the 2008 CASE/Carnegie U.S. Professor of the Year award, and producer of wildly popular online videos. He says that he, too, believes empathy is the most important skill students can master. I have also spoken with professors at West Point, who consider a broad cultural perspective one of the essential qualities they must develop in their officer candidates. Visit http://novemberlearning.com /an-interview-with-michael-wesch-part-1-of-3 for a link to a podcast with Michael Wesch and me.

When a variety of respected sources from different backgrounds and professions (and, who definitely did not study from the same set of notes) all say the same thing, I pay attention. Their message is clear for educators: we need to start teaching our students global empathy by developing their ability to understand and appreciate other points of view. In the Digital Learning Farm model, the student role of global communicator and collaborator can help in this process.

When the web was first developed, I imagined it would trigger an explosion of communication and collaboration around the world. With online capabilities, anyone could publish and exchange ideas with people from around the world, which I felt certain would lead to deeper global understanding. I was wrong. Google and other search engines have evolved such highly personalized functions that many web users see very limited search results, results that include only those information sources that reinforce—rather than challenge—their existing ideas and points of view.

As online organizer and author Eli Pariser explains in his 2011 TED talk, two people typing in the same search term from their own computer will receive two completely different sets of search results. (You can watch the whole talk at www.ted.com/talks/eli_pariser_beware_online_filter _bubbles.html.)

In his example, two different individuals issued their own Google search based on the single word *Egypt*; the first one received results connected to travel sites in Egypt, while the other's search results revolved almost exclusively around the Arab Spring uprising. One search term and two different searchers yield two totally different sets of search results.

As Eli outlines in his talk, Google and many other online search tools use what are called *personalized search algorithms*, search "rule sets" that mine past online behavior and other individual data points (the type of computer you're using, the location of the computer, and so on) to anticipate the type of material you will be most interested in seeing from the web. These types of personalized search results can seriously limit our exposure to ideas and information that fall outside our current worldview or other frame of reference. If we aren't aware of the filters that determine the nature of information we find in Internet searches, we can easily believe that ours is the only viewpoint that matters—or even exists! When that happens, our capacity for empathy and understanding can suffer, as can our ability to communicate and collaborate with others. What irony that the most global and democratic of all sources of information, the Internet, can be turned into a highly biased and personalized results list depending on your past search history!

Without some real education about using the Internet for communicating and collaborating with an authentic, global audience, this marvelously rich medium will only narrow—not broaden—our perspective. That is just one of the reasons why I've added the job of global communicator and collaborator to my list of important student contributions in the Digital Learning Farm model.

With Internet access so readily available in most of our classrooms, it would seem logical to connect our students to the world and to provide them with the authentic experiences of working with people from different cultures. In some schools, this type of collaboration is already happening. For example, I watched students in New York City exchange notes for a play they were writing, a story based in Buckingham

Palace with students in London. Their excitement at receiving edits to their narrative from British students far surpassed the power a similar critique from their teacher in their own classroom would have carried.

Everyone Benefits From a Global Perspective

As an educator, are you interested in expanding your own global perspective? There's no better way to do that than to join in conversation and collaboration with educators from around the world. Skype and the other communication tools discussed in this chapter offer teachers an inexpensive opportunity to collaborate with teachers in other countries and to share ideas and issues that shape their approach to the educational process.

The ePals site (www.epals.com), for example, offers K–12 educators an opportunity to meet and collaborate with their peers in what the site's operators call "the world's largest K–12 social learning network." While educators from around the globe are using the ePals site for global communication and collaboration, educators in the United States have been a bit late to the table. The site's founder shared with me that the United States doesn't even rank in the top twenty-five countries whose educators have partnered with their foreign counterparts on the site. As more teachers take advantage of this and other opportunities for global networking, the United States will become better equipped to help students develop a broader global perspective and a more informed understanding of the world we share.

Some educators and schools in the United States have already begun broadening their students' world understanding by creating and implementing marvelous programs that emphasize long-distance collaboration and communication. In a school near Oklahoma City, in every class from kindergarten to fifth grade, every teacher partners with another teacher in a classroom located in another country to bring their students together in collaborative projects and study groups. As you learn in this chapter, Silvia Tolisano and her colleagues at the Martin J. Gottlieb Day School in Jacksonville, Florida, have incorporated the work of global communicator and collaborator in their educational programs—just one of many jobs for student contributors in their classrooms.

Brad Ovenell-Carter (of the THINK Global School) offers two very compelling reasons to build the work of global communicator and collaborator into your students' classroom experiences: "First, you can do it. It's so easy to Skype with another classroom. As long as someone has one computer with a camera on it, you're good to go. You can crowd a bunch of kids around a table and they're all happy to poke their heads in from the side, and away you go."

He goes on to say, "Secondly—and again, it's part of letting go of control—as a teacher, I begin to learn so much more. I know I've been teaching my way, and living in Canada and the west, I've seen the world from one particular viewpoint. But when you have a kid pipe up and say, 'Hang on a second, my cousin lives in Israel, and I have a different point of view on this whole thing,' it just makes the discussion that much richer. If we believe the point of schooling is to either solve a problem or get a better understanding of the problem, then I think we have to believe that we need a lot of voices in on that problem, and we're in great danger if we're only listening to our own."

Any classroom can be organized to be a global communications center, and we can design more rigorous and motivating assignments that engage our students to collaborate globally with purpose. Now let's examine the way today's pioneering educators are leading their students to become more sophisticated users of online tools for global communication and research, and more skillful collaborators with people outside their classroom, their age group, and their local and national communities. I will also outline some simple steps for using a few widely available tools that aid educators as they guide students in their work as global communicators and collaborators.

The Story: Students Take Their Place in the Global Forum

As you learned in chapter 3, Silvia Tolisano is a 21st century learning specialist at the Martin J. Gottlieb Day School in Jacksonville, Florida. There, as students take part in a variety of jobs inspired by the idea that they are contributors on the Digital Learning Farm, they are encouraged to take more leadership roles in their own learning. We have seen how some classes in Silvia's school are using the work of student scribes to engage students more meaningfully in classroom discussions and to aid student learning and performance. I spoke with Silvia and her team of head teachers, colleagues, and students about the other types of jobs students perform at the Gottlieb Day School, including that of global communicator and collaborator. That work opens the doors for a multitude of other student contributions to the learning experience. At the same time, it makes the Skype video conference a much richer and more valuable tool for teaching students the nuts and bolts of virtual learning and collaboration.

"In our case," Silvia explains, "when we started Skype video conferencing with lots of different schools or experts about a subject area, or from a different country, it was a natural thing to do to give each student a different kind of job. We really didn't know what [work] each student would like or what they would gravitate toward. Later, we found out that [some] were really good at editing, and some were wonderful in being able to listen to a conversation and then summarize it. Others, loved to

be more in the background, documenting [the conversations] with video or with a digital camera." That *back channel* work is critical to managing the classroom conversations and questions that occur while the Skype conference is in progress.

Todaysmeet.com is a website that enables users to create a virtual classroom, select a topic, and determine the appropriate duration of the discussion of that topic. With regard to using that particular website, Silvia notes, "While a conversation is happening in the forefront—the video conference—students are asking questions and receiving answers. The back channelers are on a computer, documenting what is happening. Later on the class blog, the back channel cleanup person can download the back channel log to our class blog." In addition to cleaning up and condensing multiple back-channel notes, the cleanup crew also flags any information that they think may be incorrect, so the class can check it out. So the Skype conference is not only bringing multiple perspectives and outside expert content to the classroom, but the work of recording and posting it also teaches students to summarize and synthesize information.

Shelly Zavon, a fifth-grade general studies teacher at the school, has identified as many as twelve different student jobs that fall within the work of global communicator and collaborator in her classroom: "It starts with easy things like [maintaining] the calendar and [determining] what date we're going to Skype with another school. Then [there's] the greeter, who is the one who says hello once we make the Skype connection. And then we go to the sharer, who tells a little bit about Jacksonville and the school. We have the interviewers who do the questions and answers. They have to prepare in advance; we always like to see their questions [beforehand] to make sure they're relevant to the call that we're making. We have a photographer who takes still pictures. We have a videographer who records everything on the flip cam. [And] we have the back channelers."

Silvia and her team always ask students to volunteer for the work involved in these cross-location video conferences, and they have no trouble filling every task. She says, "The hands pop up like you just wouldn't believe. They want to do everything. And when they don't get a job, they make us write down their names for the next time that we Skype so they can make sure that they get a job."

Teachers, of course, are busy people whose time is incredibly valuable. I asked Silvia and her team about the challenge of introducing new concepts, such as the work of global communicator and collaborator, into their classroom. Was it overwhelming to have to adopt new tools and a different pedagogy? Or did the whole thing come naturally to them?

Silvia and her team say that no, this kind of globally oriented classroom work didn't come naturally to them at all. As Shelly notes, however, the teaching staff didn't have to worry about mastering complicated technologies. "To be perfectly honest," she says, "the children, the students, know so much about computers these days that once we introduced what we were doing, they basically did everything for us. There's very little learning that the teacher has to do. The students tell us things that we don't know how to do. They're incredible." Again, some educators may have trouble giving up the idea that they have to bring all the answers to the table, but allowing students to take more control of the collaborative tools and processes gives them an even greater learning experience.

Those students who spoke with me said their work as global communicator and collaborator had taught them to take on responsibility and to "have everything in order." All of them were looking forward to continuing their work the next year. Their ongoing experience with this job will become even richer as they move on to upper-level grades, because Silvia and her colleagues also engage their students in projects that involve collaboration between grade levels within the school.

Judy Reppert's eighth-grade social studies class, for example, took on the responsibility of demonstrating the techniques of good interviewing to the fifth-grade class. Judy's class was studying the geography of Central and Southern America when Silvia learned of a young man who was traveling through those areas on his way to Antarctica (as part of a project associated with National Geographic). The eighth-grade class arranged to interview the explorer via Skype. Judy was shocked by the way the students took ownership of the process. As they began drawing up interview questions, they pulled out atlases and scoured Google Maps to locate the route the young man would be taking. Then they did research to find out what political events were unfolding in the areas he'd be traveling through, so they could ask him questions about the political climate. As Judy describes it, "It wasn't just question and answer. It was an enormous spurt of learning that went into creating the questions in the interviews just for the Skyping. It has created for me the desire to create more such experiences for the students and let them take ownership of what they were learning, and it let them get excited about what might be unexpected for me as a teacher."

Through Shelly Zavon's fifth-grade students' participation in this process, they learned valuable skills in going beyond the basics of the geography involved in other areas, to researching the social, cultural, and political landscapes as well. Shelly's students were the project's back channelers, but they became so excited by the work that they wanted to be part of the interview process as well. Shelly explains that the eighth graders would be doing all of the actual interviewing, but her students weren't willing to be sidelined: "So they formulated their own questions, and bombarded Silvia. They said that they had their own questions and they wanted to ask them." Seeing how much work these fifth-grade students had done on their own, with no prompting or assignments from their teachers, Shelly and Judy relented and allowed them to pose some of their questions at the end of the interview. "They did it on their own because they wanted to," Shelly added."

The experiences of these students and their teachers emphasize the power of connecting students to an authentic audience, and the potential for students to participate in rich, meaningful work with groups outside their age level, experience, and nationality. If we want our students to be competitive in the global economy, we must challenge them to communicate *to* and collaborate *with* a worldwide authentic audience. As Silvia's team demonstrates, by guiding our students in the work of global communicators and collaborators, we can expand the boundaries of their potential and give them the courage and broader social understanding they need to engage successfully with the world. This work helps students learn to evaluate ideas from multiple perspectives, develop better understanding of issues, become better at rooting out problems and creating solutions that work for everyone.

Publishing to a Global Audience

When my daughter Jessie was about fourteen, she was a huge Harry Potter fan. When a new book was released, we would stand in line at midnight at the bookstore, and Jessie would start reading the book in the car on the way home. By breakfast the next day, she was finished. Then came the inevitable question, "Daddy, how long before J. K. Rowling writes another one?" Finally, Jessie learned to fill the long pause between Hogwarts sagas by reading a website called www.fanfiction.net. There, budding authors submit their own stories about characters and settings from popular fiction, many carefully written in the style of the original author. Jessie voraciously read submissions that revolved around the stories of J. K. Rowling.

Although I encouraged Jessie to submit her own work, she decided she was a better critic than a fiction writer. She even decided she would give out her own Pulitzer-like annual award for excellence to www.fanfiction.net writers. Jessie announced on the site that she would bestow the Golden Cauldron award to the best J. K. Rowling–like author. I asked her how many people she had on her review committee. She proudly responded, "Just me, Daddy. I am the Golden Cauldron."

Of course, I asked my daughter if she would share the work she was judging, and I quickly became fascinated by the amazing writing skill of Jessie's finalists. I even began to include examples from young www.fanfiction.net writers in my workshops for teachers to demonstrate that if you give students a worldwide audience, some students will exceed our expectations for quality and quantity. One day, I was at an independent school giving a presentation to students and teachers. When I showed one young author's creative work, a buzz began at the front of the auditorium. The author of the work I was showing, an eighth-grade girl, was in the third row! I was stunned at the odds of running into her at one of my workshops. I asked her to come up to the stage to talk about her network of favorite authors and the hundreds of comments she had received from adoring fans from around the world.

After the presentation, I was quite surprised when her teacher took me aside to tell me that the girl wasn't a particularly good student, in spite of her large body of work on www.fanfiction.net. "I'm always after her to hand in her homework," she added. Later, that day, I had a chance to ask the student what was up with her homework. She was very clear in her response. "Every day, I have to decide if I will write for my teachers or publish to the world," she said. I realized then that the battleground for our students' time and attention was becoming more crowded, as more students every day gain access to global

continued →

publishing opportunities and an authentic audience. How do we convince them to do their homework and pay attention to the ideas, skills, and knowledge we want them to master? I see only two viable solutions: we can try to cut them off from global access, or we can co-opt the media they're drawn to and include the opportunity for global publishing in our classes.

Tools and Techniques: Guiding Students to Become Global Learners

I once had to head to England on July 3 for a conference later that week. A British friend of mine picked me up at Heathrow, and I mentioned to him that I was sorry that I'd missed the Fourth of July fireworks back home. He laughed and said, "No, we don't celebrate that event in the same way here." We talked about the American Revolution as we drove into London, and I quickly came to realize that the British have a completely different version of its events—including those that sparked the war. Was the war retaliation sparked by unfair taxation by the British government, or did it stem from England's decision to abolish the financing of slave ships from West Africa? Were neither of these events key reasons for the war—or were both of them just small parts of a much larger set of issues that triggered this world-changing conflict?

In reality, there are often multiple conflicting truths about many issues. It may not be important that we all agree on a single-perspective view of any idea or issue, but it *is* important to know that those other perspectives exist. We improve both our own understanding and our ability to work with others when we gain insight into the what, why, and how of other perspectives—and learn to value them.

How do we learn about the experiences and influences of the rest of the world? One of our most commonly used tools for gathering information is the Internet. Like any tool, however, the web only works well if we know how to use it. It's important to remember that we can't broaden our perspective if we let technology do our thinking for us. Teaching our students a more sophisticated way to use search-engine technology is just one step in developing their skills at critical thinking. Web literacy isn't just about learning to be productive online; it also involves taking control of the technologies that we use, so that we—not our tools—are guiding our results. With that kind of fluency, we can tap into the Internet's rich opportunities for broadening our worldview and learning to see issues and ideas the way other people see them, even those ideas that are completely foreign to our way of thinking.

Too many of our students are learning about global history and events without the opportunity of engaging in conversation with authentic global audiences. Reading an article or a chapter from a textbook or a novel, or even seeing a film or YouTube video, are all important ways to learn more about the world around us. However, they don't provide an opportunity for the exchange of ideas. Fortunately, the widespread availability of Internet connectivity and free tools such as Skype have made it much easier and more inexpensive to speak and collaborate with other people and groups around the world.

What about that wide gap between the views that Brits and Yanks have about that little scuffle that began in 1775? Let me be the first to confess that back in my teaching days in Lexington, Massachusetts, I never taught the British point of view about "our" war. If I were in that classroom today, I'd challenge my students to find students or classrooms in England with whom they could discuss, via Skype, the ideas and events that surrounded the American Revolution. To prepare for the discussions, I would have my students use primary sources from England to research the events that led up to the conflict. I imagine that more than a few students would study harder for an upcoming debate with British students over Skype than for a written exam I might give them on Friday. Their motivation for that study would grow even more powerful if I told them that the debate would be recorded and turned into a podcast for the world to access. Perhaps I would challenge my students: "This debate is about our hard-fought right to be self-governed. Let's also win the debate."

In this section, I will outline the steps involved in using this important tool for global collaboration. But first, let me explain another simple technique for conducting targeted online searches (a method that I referenced earlier in the book) that will return results from specific groups or locations. That way, you can be certain of receiving search results that open a window into the ways other people see ideas, issues, and the world we all share.

Searching for Other Perspectives

As stated previously, unless you understand how Google actually generates results when you search, it can limit your worldview without you knowing it is happening. Search engine developers have been personalizing their algorithms to memorize our every online action and use that data bank to anticipate our interests and deliver sites specifically aimed at us. That makes shopping for those shoes you want a bit faster and easier, but it makes learning about issues from multiple perspectives much more difficult.

If you want proof of these difficulties, I offer you a challenge. Remember those disparate views of the American Revolution referenced earlier? I challenge you to go online to find information *from British school sources* about what British schools are teaching their students about that war. Do a search for "schools in England studying American Revolution," or whatever terms you choose (the British often call it the American War of Independence).

This isn't a trick question. I frequently give this problem to U.S. students. I put twenty dollars on the table and tell them, "If you can find search results that only include schools in England, I'll give you the twenty." Most students are so confident that they can use Google to find anything they want, they laugh at me—to date, they have all failed. See if you can do it. If your results aren't limited to schools in

England, maybe you made the same mistake as the students. They type in something like "schools in England studying American Revolution." I just ran this search on the computer I'm working at now; the results are shown in figure 5.1.

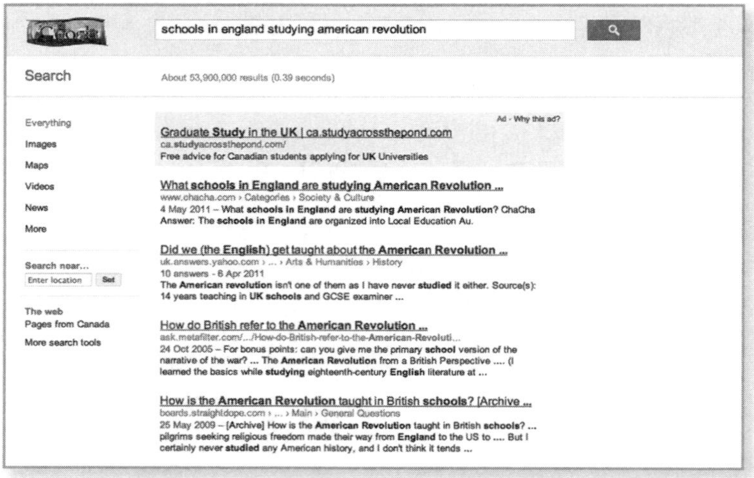

Figure 5.1: These are the results of the online search for "schools in England studying American Revolution."

It turns out that *none* of the results returned by this search come from a school in England. At this point, most school students think they're done. I have to say, "No, look at the web addresses—nothing from a school in England." (I talked about deciphering web addresses in chapter 4.) They keep going, but after about ten minutes, these students are suffering. Then I show them how to access the Root Zone database.

The Root Zone database is a reference source, something like a dictionary or thesaurus, that lists the delegation details for Internet domain names used in web addresses. It includes two-letter codes for every country in the world. UK is the code for the United Kingdom. I show students the UK listing in the database, and then return to my search page. I explain that Google, like an index or table of contents, lets you index your search results so you only see those from the specific type of location you indicate in the search. Next, in the Google search box, I type in the site: command *site:uk domain school* to find the domain code for school sites in England. The first result from that search shows that the school domain code is *sch*. Finally, I show the students my final search phrase—*site:sch.uk "American Revolution"*—and explain that the quotation marks keep the last two words together as a single term (chapter 4, page 63, has more information about using the site: command). Click the Search button, and bingo! The entire result list is made up of sources from schools within the UK (see figure 5.2).

Watch the students' faces when they see the results. Many begin to realize that they didn't know what they thought they knew about how Google really works.

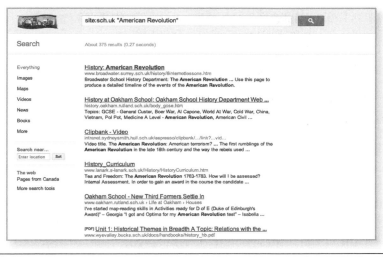

Figure 5.2: These search results include *only* sources from schools in the United Kingdom.

I have shown students how to use the site: command to search for information related to a number of academic topics—math, science, literature, and so on—and they are always surprised to learn about this tool. They typically haven't been taught in school how to use the web globally, to get results specifically sourced from another country, organization, or location's perspective. Digital literacy is included in the Common Core State Standards, adopted by the majority of states. If you are an educator, whether your students are in second or twelfth grade, you can teach them to search using the Root Zone database and the site: command to expand both their world perspectives and their web literacy. Visit its website at www.iana.org/domains/root/db/ to learn more about the Root Zone database.

Using Skype

Of all of the tools out there, Skype is probably the one that you can easily make use of on a daily basis. In a nutshell, Skype (www.skype.com) is a video conferencing service that allows users to make computer-to-computer video conference phone calls to anyone in the world absolutely free, using an Internet connection. Imagine the possibilities. We can collaborate and make global connections with family, classes, and professional peers.

To use Skype, all you need for basic service is a computer with a microphone and a set of speakers. Regular users of Skype, however, will quickly encourage you to purchase a headset with a noise-canceling microphone attached. Noise-canceling microphones eliminate a lot of background noise, and the headset will prevent the person who you are talking to from having to listen to themselves through your speakers during their conversation with you. If you don't have the money for these headphones, though, don't be discouraged. As Eric Marcos pointed out in chapter 2, the microphone that comes with most computers today will work. Beyond this, the only other thing you need is the Skype program that can be easily downloaded onto your Windows, Macintosh, or Linux computer.

Setting Up Skype

The first time you launch Skype, you will be prompted to set up your Skype account. Fill in the information, including the Skype name of your choice. This is the name others on Skype will use to get in touch with you. (I don't recommend that you use your full name.) You can find other Skype users by clicking on the magnifying glass at the top of the Skype window and searching in the window that appears for a Skype name, email address, city, state, country, and so on. When you find the other Skype user you are looking for, click Add to add that user to your Skype buddy list. On the other end, your buddy will get a message asking him or her to approve you and add you to his or her Skype list. If he or she approves you, you're in.

Here are some of the things you can do with Skype:

- **Video calls**—If you and your partner both have webcams, you can add video capabilities to your Skype calls.

- **Instant messaging**—Click on a buddy in your Skype list, and press the Chat button to chat, just as you would through any other instant messaging program.

- **File transfer**—Select a user in your buddy list, and press the Send File button (the blue arrow). Skype will prompt you to browse for the file, select it, and send it. If your buddy on the other end approves the file, Skype delivers it.

- **Conference calls**—You and up to four of your contacts can collaborate in a Skype conference call.

If you are looking for other classes to Skype with, consider visiting a classroom exchange site like ePals where you can search for other classes with whom to collaborate. Once you've chosen a class and have set up a relationship, tell the class about Skype and invite the teacher and students to join.

Here are some of the ways you can use Skype with students:

- Have world language students participate in Skype conversations with students from other countries.

- Allow students who are working on a collaborative project to participate in a conference call from various locations.

- Exchange documents with project partners.

- Have students present their work to an authentic audience—for example, to other classrooms around the world or professionals in their community.

- Let parents listen in on their child's presentation.

- Arrange an interview with an author whose book your class is reading.

- Invite a guest speaker to talk to your class via Skype.

- Invite a grandparent to share a personal story relating to history.

Recording a Skype Interview

Recording Skype interviews is a simple process. You begin by setting up your Skype account. You can download Skype from its website (www.skype.com). Install and create an account, following the instructions on the Skype site. Remember that the account name you choose will be the one you give others to use when connecting with you for an interview.

You can choose one of two ways to connect with the other party:

1. If the other person has (or will install) Skype on his or her computer, you can simply make a free Skype call to that person from your computer to his or hers.

2. Use SkypeOut to call the other party on his or her mobile or landline phone. This option is inexpensive.

For the best quality in your recording, we highly suggest the free Skype-to-Skype method and that all parties use noise-canceling microphones and headphones to cancel out unwanted echoes. You can invest in a pair of headphones with microphone at most electronics shops for as little as twenty dollars.

Follow these steps to record and edit the interview:

1. When you are ready to begin your Skype interview, call the other party. Skype allows users to make conference calls between as many as five Skype account computers (including yours). To start a conference call, open Skype, click on the Call menu, and choose Start a Conference Call on a Mac (or click the Conference button on a PC). Select the individuals you want to include on your call.

2. Once you have all parties on the line, you can start recording your conversation using a recording program (check for current rate and details for using the products at each site). On the Mac, you can use Audio Hijack (found at www.rogueamoeba.com). On a PC you can use PowerGramo (found at www .powergramo.com), or Pamela (found at www.pamela-systems.com). These programs are easy to install and include a one-button record feature. (Visit **go.solution-tree.com/instruction** for live links to the websites mentioned in this book.)

3. At the end of your call, stop the recording process. The recording program will give you the option to save your work as an MP3 file.

4. Now you can open your saved file in either Audacity (it is Mac- and PC-compatible, http://audacity.sourceforge.net) or GarageBand (Mac only, www.apple.com/ilife/garageband) to edit your interview if you choose. Once the edits are complete, simply upload your newly edited file to your website, blog, or podcast series. Advertise the interview to other classes and peers, and encourage feedback.

A Short Q&A About the Process

Here are some of the questions I commonly ask (or am asked) about implementing the work of student global communicator and collaborator in the classroom, along with some of the answers I've given and received.

Question: When you adopt this job, or any student job, is there a period of transition and adjustment?

Answer: As with many new classroom approaches, educators and students will need some time to take on their new roles and become comfortable with the new technologies and processes involved in Skyping and conducting targeted searches. As the teaching team from the Martin J. Gottlieb Day School has discovered, students tend to be eager to get involved in this role, and their native technical skills can help ease the learning curve.

Question: What kinds of assistants or mentors can be helpful in guiding the class as students take on the role of global communicator and collaborator?

Answer: Fifth-grade teacher Shelly Zavon recommends that educators involve two or three mentors to help guide students in this work. Her team drew upon the advice of a computer teacher and Silvia Tolisano, who was spearheading the student jobs program at the school. Educators may have other mentor options available to them, such as a technology support person or librarian. As Shelly notes, being willing to communicate and collaborate with other professionals and resources is a critical step in teaching those same skills to your students. She says, "You have to be able to ask for help, you have to be able to collaborate, and you have to be able to accept that you may fail sometimes with what you do—and just go with it. Go to Plan B if it doesn't work out with Plan A."

We have talked about a number of ways that we can create and incorporate student contributions through specific jobs, including those of tutorial designer, student scribe, student researcher, and global communicator and collaborator. In the final chapter of this book, we'll look at how some educators are combining these and other student jobs in their own versions of the Digital Learning Farm model. Before we move on, however, let's take a moment to consider a few important questions about introducing the work of global communicator and collaborator into that model.

Questions for Discussion

1. What kinds of opportunities can you imagine for enabling students to engage with authentic audiences around the world?

2. In what ways do you believe that assignments that challenge students to partner with students globally can be more motivating for students than teacher-assigned grades?

3. What reasons might discourage educators from leveraging our investment in the Internet to engage students in authentic global learning experiences?

4. What barriers do you anticipate educators will face in guiding students in the role of global communicator and collaborator?

6

Joining Forces in Purposeful Work: The Legacy of Student Contribution

In each of the preceding chapters, we have seen the educational power and motivational force of purposeful work and student contribution in the classroom. We learned how Eric Marcos and his sixth-grade class have leveraged the benefits of students teaching students as they explore the possibilities of students as tutorial designers. We looked at the work of Darren Kuropatwa's high school math class in creating and collecting course notes and diagrams on its own educational blog as we examined the job of student scribe. Finally, we learned how Silvia Tolisano and her colleagues have linked their students with other learners, educators, and topic experts around the globe in the rich experience of becoming global communicators and collaborators. Individually, these jobs offer students exceptional learning benefits, but their true power for creating 21st century learners comes together in a Digital Learning Farm model that embraces all of these opportunities for student contribution. But what would that model look like, and how would it work?

In this chapter, we are going to listen to Garth Holman (a middle school teacher from Beachwood, Ohio) and his partner and colleague Michael Pennington (seventh -grade history teacher from Chardon, Ohio) talk about their experiences in guiding students to build the students' wiki, a digital online history textbook. These two teachers have inspired their students to do their own research, create their own lesson content, develop their own teaching tools, and collaborate with each other, with other students, and with content experts from around the world to build an online digital textbook. In the process, these students have created a digital footprint—a teaching and learning legacy that will live on even when the original contributors have moved on into college and beyond.

As with many of the examples in this book, the story you are about to read comes from a conversation I had with Garth and Michael, which was recorded for my website. Here, the story recorded in that conversation *is* the chapter's message, not just one illustration of it. Garth and Michael offer a positive and compelling example of how student contribution to purposeful work can transform a traditional classroom into a vibrant, engaging learning environment and lead to student mastery of a subject.

The students you learn about here have worked hard and exceeded expectations in their dedicated pursuit of learning, creativity, collaboration, and innovation. No points received, no grades involved; the students do this work because it matters, to them and to others. Yes, these teachers and their students have worked hard on this project, and not every educator will want to re-create this project or will be able to match this investment of time and energy. But all of us can benefit from seeing how these two teachers and their students, using limited resources and boundless initiative, have created an exciting model of what the digital learning experience can be, and the incredible educational results it can achieve.

A Student Wiki—and Legacy—Is Born

Garth and Michael had been collaborating with their students in the creation of The Students' History, a digital online wiki world history textbook located at http:// dgh.wikispaces.com (see figure 6.1), for five years when I spoke with them in December of 2010. I asked them to tell me about the project's origins. Garth and Michael discuss their project on their professional website Teachers for Tomorrow (www.teachersfortomorrow.net).

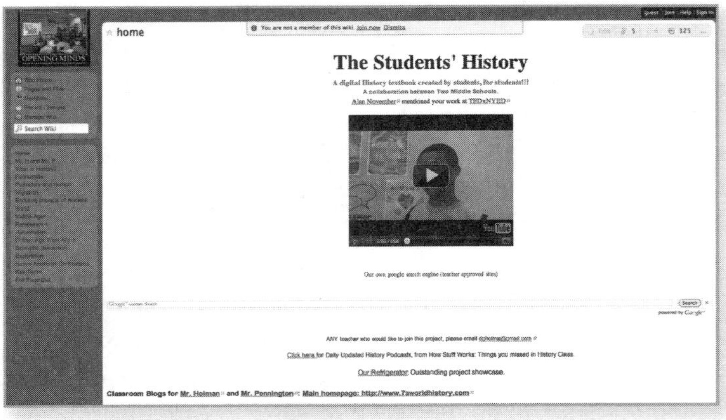

Figure 6.1: Seventh-grade students from two schools in Ohio collaborated on this digital online world history textbook.

Source: Holman & Pennington, 2011. Used with permission.

Garth says, "This started in 2006 when Mike was student teaching with me at Beachwood, and I had this idea that with technology, we should be able to create our own content. And so, that first year he was there, Mike signed on to the very end of the year, even though he was finished, and we were going to try to see how far we could get with kids building a wiki. We got a base of written information from the kids, and we put that into a wiki the first year. And in the second year when we started school, we took a look at the book with the kids and they're like, 'Well, it's no different from our book. It's just text.' The kids said, 'We need to add hyperlinks. We need to add things in there.' And I said, 'Well, that's what we're going to do at the end of the year.' So we learned our content, and at the end of the year kids picked topics they were most interested in, and they began to write formal papers for it."

Garth goes on to say, "If you go back and look at the history of the pages when they first started [their wiki provides a History tab that lists every version of every page from the very first entry], we just took our standards for what we were supposed to be teaching, divided them up, and let the kids go, so we could see what they would create. The first year, we got very little. By the second year, we had a substantial amount of information for our entire course. We continue to just add to it each year. We've branched out in the kind of information we started to add into it, but we still have kids editing. This week, kids were editing it and making changes to the original text that was put in there."

Michael Pennington adds, "I think it's also important to point out that when we started this project, it was almost a paper-based review of the year. We tried to break up what we had looked at in different areas of history. Then we really just let the kids pick what they wanted to do. Upfront, they knew that they were doing the project for intrinsic learning, if you want to use that phrase. Students knew that it was going to go online and it was going to stay there, but they knew they weren't going to get points for the work. From the beginning, it's been students doing it because they want to leave that digital footprint."

I mentioned to Michael and Garth that author Daniel Pink says that the more we grade children on creative work, the less they'll do. I asked these two teachers what motivating force they believed to be behind their students' contributions to the wiki. Did they think their students were motivated by the value-adding nature of their work and its benefits for other kids?

Garth immediately responds that he has seen the work's long-term legacy empower his students, and that empowerment holds the key to their motivation: "It empowers them because it lives on. It lives on after they've moved through seventh grade. Now they're into high school and some kids are approaching college, and their book is still there, and they can see their original text, where it started, and how it's morphed. I think that motivates kids. Daniel Pink has it right when he gives the idea that if you truly get creative work, points don't matter. It's when the work is mundane that the points matter." Michael adds, "There's a definite ownership in this work."

Driving Collaborative, Lifelong Learning

To further eliminate the mundane from his class's learning experience, Michael says he had been implementing a no-homework policy in his classroom. No homework? Really? I asked him if parents were complaining. "I haven't heard complaints about no homework because of the large amounts of homework that students already have. Actually, I get a lot of compliments and thank-yous." In his community, which he describes as "rural borderline," parents are able to see the benefits of allowing his student-created research, tutorials, and content to take the place of rote memorization work. Garth has had the same experience in his smaller community. I asked him if the wiki would someday replace his textbook. He says it already has to some degree. He says, "The textbook was sent home the first month of school, and I tell the kids to leave it at home, not to bring it to school, that if we need one, there'll be a class set. We use it occasionally, mostly for looking at images, not really for a lot of text reading. In the last project we were doing, where the kids were working on the enduring impacts of the ancient world, their resources included the online textbook, the Internet, with some preprovided sources we gave them, and inspiration where they're building labs. So, the textbook is the secondary source in my classroom, if not third or fourth source."

With so many kids reading each other's work, I wondered if they offered a lot of feedback for improving the wiki's content. I asked Garth if this was a really collaborative process, or if the students stick to their own sections.

Garth says, "Originally, kids were working in pairs or groups of three to do a page, and so we basically gave them a standard and a blank page and said, 'Here's your page. You need to decide what to put on it, what to add, what needs to go there.' As you look through the book, you see some pages that are pretty text driven. You see some with YouTube videos embedded, and others where the kids embedded their own podcasts. In June, at the end of the school year, I have kids adding in podcasts they made in November. The online textbook is almost always updated the last two to three days of school when the kids are really putting their final pieces in. So unlike most schools, the kids at Beachwood Middle School spend the last two days of school writing their textbook that lives on. Their last few days in seventh grade are about getting their work published."

Garth continues: "Mike and I are just kind of playing. We're taking risks every year. What can we do now? How do we do this now? We began this with a seven- to ten-year vision. We had this idea of where we wanted to get to, and we weren't sure how to get there so we just said, 'Let's get the standards down and move on.' Well, this year we did some Google Doc work where we looked at all of the topics that we'd addressed throughout the year, and the kids in my classes began to randomly add what they remembered about these topics. All along, the kids in Mike's class thirty-six miles away were watching that Google Doc develop—kind of eavesdropping. Then, Mike's kids Skyped in during the last five minutes of class and said, 'Here are things that you forgot that need to be added.' So we took all that information, and I said to the kids, 'Look, the text base is pretty good in the book, but we need somebody to edit. We need podcasts, we need iMovies, and we need cartoons.' So the kids began to say, 'You know what, I really like cartooning. I want to do a political cartoon for the online book.' Once again, they're using higher-level thinking skills to create a visual image to represent the content that's written in text. They're truly building; they're constructing their own knowledge as we go. But it's the process between our two classes, in schools thirty-six miles apart, that is just as interesting, if not more interesting."

I asked Michael what synergies he thought would be lost in this process if the collaboration between the two classes wasn't part of it. He says, "I think that it would almost lose its impact entirely, especially for the kids. Every day that I come in, I have half a dozen (if not more) kids asking when we're going to Skype with Beachwood that week: 'Why didn't we get to it yet? Why are we not doing this? Why are we not doing that?' Their ability to see that their learning isn't just happening in this little room for the sake of me is astounding. They want to impress the kids from Beachwood. They want to show Beachwood that they want to collaborate on projects. It's beyond what any academic standard can tell you; you need to teach in your classroom, but it's probably the most important thing that we're doing."

Garth adds, "Yes, if you take away Mike from this equation, then the whole project loses the basis of what's really happening. Every day, Mike and I are modeling this collaborative effort through Skype, through Google Docs. We do what we call 'computer side chats' that we post up for the kids. In them, he and I just have a conversation on Skype about the topics we're studying. Then, the kids are commenting on the blog about how valuable it is to hear two adults talk about the topics the kids are studying, to hear perceptions of the adults. So we are consistently modeling everything we're talking about, then building."

"They talk a ton about leaving digital footprints for other people to find," Garth continues. "So through the beginning of the year when we teach media listening, we do stuff with Facebook and we do stuff with Twitter, and explain how these things work and how you find information. How does Google choose search results? Why is a site number one, number two? The kids grasp that, but then they see Mike and I continue to use that process all year; it adds so much more to their experience at the end of the year, when they're building this book. It's the culmination of thirty-six weeks of work, and I say that because it's not just the text. To me, the online book is not what's important. The book is the final product that you can see, but it's the interaction of these kids going on every day and the way they're seeing the use of technology-engaged learning and how technology changes the way we learn and the way the world works that I think is the most valuable the end product. In reality, it's also that interaction every day that is changing learning in our classrooms."

Michael agrees, "The kids are realizing that learning is a natural process of life. It happens and it should be happening all the time, and as long as you are aware of it, you're going to get so much more out of it."

Spreading the Medium and the Message

With all of the excitement and success Michael and Garth have generated with their student-created wiki textbook, I wondered if other teachers in their school systems had launched similar projects.

Garth admits that none of the other teachers at his school had tackled this specific kind of work, but he adds, "There's actually a lot going on. I've got teachers in my building who, at one point, were Skyping weekly. Their middle school kids are reading once a week to the kindergarteners in a district forty-five miles away via Skype. We've also have people using some of the blogging spaces for the kids to build on. You're seeing more and more of this web 2.0 stuff where the kids are able to create. They just want their kids to be engaged in learning in a way that's different from the traditional approach."

I told Michael and Garth that these examples sounded like projects, where their work was actually a whole new approach to teaching. How did they come up with this seven-to-ten-year vision whereas, at least in my observation, so many other educators are addressing change with a single project at a time?

Michael explains, "Part of it really began with my blind luck at being placed in Garth's classroom as a student teacher. I had to learn very quickly to teach in a different manner than I had been learning in my college classes. We're both extremely hardworking, reflective people. I would say that there wasn't a single day that went by while I was a student teacher that we didn't spend at least an hour talking about what we were doing that day and how it could be better. I think those reflective conversations are what spurred us on to look even longer term at what we're creating, not only for our kids we're teaching right now, but how was that going to impact the next group of kids and then the next group of kids, and how is that going to impact us as educators. Garth, had eight or nine years in teaching, and I was just starting my career, and we could see these huge changes that were happening. We didn't want our kids to fall behind the eight ball. We wanted them to be out in front, to be leaders. During those individual periods of reflection, we realized that we needed to plan on a grander scale."

"Reflecting on my own education while growing up, I don't remember any of my tests," Garth adds. "I don't remember any of my multiple-choice tests or my written answers. But I remember the experiences that I had. I kept thinking about those experiences and wondering what can we give the kids that's an experience that they typically don't get, other than in a one-day cultural fair or something. What's the experience that we can give kids that will last the rest of their lives? And I knew it had to be something that doesn't end, where what they do continues on."

"And they love it!" Michael says. "They love the idea that next year's students might be using their work to study for a test or to learn about a topic."

Garth continues, "I've had at least five different students that have contacted me and said, 'Hey, Mr. Holman, I noticed you're missing this page. Over the summer, can I build that for you?' I'm not one to turn down free help so I said, 'Sure!' They'll email me and say, 'Have you got some resources I can read before I start this? Where do you want me to look?' I'm amazed at how many kids are anxious to do work to get it on there. I have a kid right now who told me, 'I'd like to do an iMovie that I can put on the online book to introduce all students to the topic before they do any reading.' I'm like, 'Well, that makes a lot of sense to me—go do it.' He's working on the iMovie now. And I think that every summer for the past four years, I've had students engaged in the book on their own time outside of school."

How often do your students feel such a compelling sense of responsibility that they will spend time during summer vacation to rewrite work from the previous school year?

Garth goes on to say, "I called Mike over Thanksgiving weekend. I'm like, 'Dude, something's going on. There are like 900 edits to our online book.' We leave it open, and there were some classes in California that had been looking at it, commenting on the book, adding and changing information in the book—all of which has been appropriate. I don't see anything wrong with it; in fact, I'm intrigued by it. I originally shut the book down every day. But I talked to the kids about it. I said, 'There were so many edits, I can't keep up with them. I don't know who is changing what.' The kids said, 'Isn't that the point?' And I said, 'Absolutely.' So right then and there, we opened it back up while they were sitting in the classroom, and now it's still opened."

Garth continues, "That's the beauty of open source: it's there. I think the process of education is collaboration. The idea of school should be collaboration and communication with people that are different from you and see the world with different eyes. So the involvement of more people that who see the world differently than my kids at Beachwood or Mike's kids at Chardon, and have a different perspective on these events, that's what education is about."

Michael adds that they hope their students' wiki is a portal for other educators and classes around the world to enter into this type of ongoing, organic learning. "It can be as simple as these teachers finding the website and just doing their own editions, or if they want to get involved with Skype talks with us, or even use Google Doc and make it a collaborative issue, we're open for anything."

Garth explains that they've already begun some of that work. "We've actually just today agreed to do a Skype-in with a middle school in Syracuse, New York, whose people have asked if we can Skype in to one of their staff meetings and talk to them a little bit about how we're using the web and the Internet to engage students in learning. We've also had contact with a guy outside of Philadelphia who is interested in doing something very similar with some of his staff. I mean, we want to see education change. That's been our goal. That's my passion. I have little kids. I want what they experience to be something different than what I experienced."

Before we ended our conversation, I congratulated Michael and Garth on the progress they've made in changing the way many students and educators look at the educational process. Their project offers a pioneering example of the impact of purposeful work and student contribution on student motivation and learning. In a time when many teachers are scrambling to find ways to make the best use of their limited time and budgets, these two remarkable educators offer a solution that accomplishes both of those goals. Teachers gain the benefit of collaborative work in their classrooms that requires only easy-to-use resources that are cheap or even freely available; their students get to invest their time in creating a useful learning tool, rather than in doing rote memorization; parents gain by being able to follow their children's work without the necessity of pushing them to finish their homework, and all of us gain the benefit of a group of students who are trained in the 21st century skills of collaboration, innovation, and the skillful use of information and communication technologies.

These are just some of the reasons that all of us can be enormously grateful for the work of Michael Pennington, Garth Holman, and their middle school students. These educators and others like them are opening the door for others to join them in building the future.

I hope this book has been successful in introducing you to the ideas that form the framework of the Digital Learning Farm model. I know that the educators and students you've read about have offered exciting examples of just how successful it can be to institute the student work that serves as the foundation for this model, and how powerful the motivating force of student contribution can be in the educational experience. Now I would like to ask you to consider some critical questions about how you might take your own first steps in putting these ideas to work.

Questions for Discussion

1. What opportunities can you identify for incorporating multiple student jobs into your classroom activities?

2. How could you help your students create an educational legacy that would outlast their own student experiences?

3. Michael and Garth explain that they could not have triggered the quality of student work their classes have achieved without tackling a project that incorporated multiple student roles. What would it take for you to be willing to undertake a massive creative project that includes the input of classrooms from outside your school—or around the world?

4. Michael and Garth also explain that ongoing, yearlong collaboration between classrooms is essential to the quality of student work. How would you structure yearlong collaboration with colleagues beyond your classroom to add value to your students' learning experiences?

Epilogue

The stories in this book illustrate that teaching our students to fully leverage 21st century skills in information and communication technologies extends well beyond introducing them to new tools. More importantly, these stories demonstrate that we are experiencing an essential change in the culture of teaching and learning. When students are given the opportunity to have purpose and ownership in their work, we see amazing things happen with the quality of their learning experiences and outcomes. We need more educational leaders and frontline teachers who are willing to empower students to co-create curriculum, own their learning, and make contributions to the collaborative process of learning. I hope *Who Owns the Learning?* will help encourage that work.

I also hope you will join the pioneering educators who are finding new, meaningful ways to promote the kinds of educational experiences you have read about here. With the more creative and rigorous work of the Common Core State Standards, teachers will have more of an incentive to link student legacy to core curricular goals. Expanding the boundaries of our classrooms to include the engagement of global authentic audiences can help us achieve results that are directly linked to existing standards.

We especially need our school leaders to support the kind of pioneering work that may at times appear to be contradictory to the traditional roles of teaching and learning. Eric Williams, the superintendent of York County Schools in Virginia, identified the link between student achievement and ownership of the learning experience when he told me of the students in his school who had created videos to teach content and skills to other students: "They wanted to get it right because they knew that these Animoto videos that they were creating were going to be viewed by their peers, not only in their class but outside of their class, in their school and others. So you talk about who owns the learning, those kids owned that."

As you have seen, in the Digital Learning Farm model, the teacher remains vitally important. While there are digital tools and new classroom management skills that some teachers will have to learn, the transition has huge benefits for your students. I suggest bringing some students with you to staff development meetings, and they will be more than willing to help implement new technologies in your classroom. Once you launch the student as contributor or global communicator and collaborator, you will see your students "stand on your shoulders." It is an amazingly rewarding professional experience.

References and Resources

Cassidy, K. (n.d.). *Mrs. Cassidy's classroom blog* [Web log]. Accessed at http://classblogmeister.com/blog.php?blogger_id=1337 on December 6, 2011.

Cook, W. (1995). *Strategic planning in America's schools*. Alexandria, VA: American Association of School Administrators.

Dewey, J. (n.d.). *BrainyQuote*. Accessed at www.brainyquote.com/quotes/authors /j/john_dewey.html on March 28, 2012.

Friedman, T. (2005). *The world is flat: A brief history of the twenty-first century*. New York: Farrar, Straus and Giroux.

Gorman, M. (2011a). *Twelve reasons to teach searching techniques with Google advanced search . . . Even before using the basic search* [Web log post]. Accessed at http://novemberlearning.com/twelve-reasons-to-teach -searching-techniques-with-google-advanced-search%E2%80%A6-even -before-using-the-basic-search on December 6, 2011.

Gorman, M. (2011b). *21st century educational technology and learning* [Web log]. Accessed at http://21centuryedtech.wordpress.com on December 6, 2011.

Holman, G., & Pennington, M. (2011, December). *The students' history* [Web log]. Accessed at http://dgh.wikispaces.com on December 1, 2011.

Holman, G., & Pennington, M. (n.d.). *Teachers for tomorrow* [Web log]. Accessed at www.teachersfortomorrow.net on January 9, 2012.

Kuropatwa, D. (n.d.). *A difference* [Web log]. Accessed at http://adifference .blogspot.com on December 6, 2011.

November, A. (2008). *Web literacy for educators*. Thousand Oaks, CA: Corwin Press.

November, A. (2010a). *Student scribes with Darren Kuropatwa—Part 1 of 3* [Video file]. Accessed at http://novemberlearning.com/student-scribes-with -darren-kuropatwa-%e2%80%93-part-1-of-3 on December 6, 2011.

November, A. (2010b). *Student scribes with Darren Kuropatwa—Part 2 of 3* [Video file]. Accessed at http://novemberlearning.com/student-scribes-with -darren-kuropatwa-part-2-of-3 on December 6, 2011.

November, A. (2010c). *Student scribes with Darren Kuropatwa—Part 3 of 3* [Video file]. Accessed at http://novemberlearning.com/student-scribes-with -darren-kuropatwa-part-3-of-3 on December 6, 2011.

November, A. (2011). *November learning*. Accessed at http://novemberlearning .com on December 6, 2011.

Pariser, E. (2011). *Beware online "Filter bubbles"* [Web log post]. Accessed at www.ted.com/talks/eli_pariser_beware_online_filter_bubbles.html on December 6, 2011.

Pink, D. (2009). *Drive: The surprising truth about what motivates us.* New York: Riverhead Books.

Polite, R. (2011, December). *Google custom search engine* [Web log]. Accessed at http://www.customsearchengine.com on December 1, 2011.

Scribe hall of fame. (n.d.). [Web log]. Accessed at http://thescribepost.pbworks .com/w/page/22148105/HallOfFame on December 6, 2011.

Sprankle, B. (2006). *Room 208 VODCAST: 04.03.06* [Video file]. Accessed at www .bobsprankle.com/blog/C1697218367/E630200618/index.html on December 6, 2011.

Sprankle, B. (n.d.a). *Bit by bit* [Web log]. Accessed at http://bobsprankle.com /bitbybit_wordpress on December 6, 2011.

Sprankle, B. (n.d.b). *Room 208* [Web log]. Accessed at www.bobsprankle.com/blog /index.html on December 6, 2011.

Valenza, J. (2011). *Truth, lies, and the Internet* [Web log post]. Accessed at http://blog.schoollibraryjournal.com/neverendingsearch/2011/10/04 /truth-lies-and-the-internet on December 6, 2011.

Warlick, D. (n.d.). *2¢ worth: Teaching and learning in the new information landscape* [Web log]. Accessed at http://davidwarlick.com/2cents on December 6, 2011.

Index

Teaching the iGeneration (2nd Edition)
William M. Ferriter and Adam Garry

Find the natural overlap between the work you already believe in and the digital tools that define today's learning. Each chapter introduces an enduring life skill and a digital solution to enhance traditional skill-based instructional practices. A collection of handouts and supporting materials ends each chapter.

BKF671

Creating a Digital-Rich Classroom
Meg Ormiston

Design and deliver standards-based lessons in which technology plays an integral role. This book provides a research base and practical strategies for using web 2.0 tools to create engaging lessons that transform and enrich content.

BKF385

21st Century Readiness for Every Student
Ken Kay

The term *21st century education* is used to describe myriad trends. In this keynote, Ken argues that for the term to have meaning, 21st century education must be rooted in knowledge and skills that ensure readiness for every student.

DVF056

Bringing Innovation to School
Suzie Boss

Activate your students' creativity and problem-solving potential with breakthrough learning projects. Across all grades and content areas, student-driven, collaborative projects will teach students how to generate innovative ideas and then put them into action.

BKF546

Solution Tree | Press
a division of
Solution Tree

Visit solution-tree.com or call 800.733.6786 to order.